Emotional Eating

A Practical Guide to Taking Control

Edward Abramson

LEXINGTON BOOKS
An Imprint of Macmillan, Inc.
New York

Maxwell Macmillan Canada
Toronto

Maxwell Macmillan International
New York Oxford Singapore Sydney

Library of Congress Cataloging-in-Publication Data

Emotional eating : a practical guide to taking control / Edward
Abramson.
p.   cm.
Includes bibliographical references.
ISBN 0-02-900215-X
1. Compulsive eating—Popular works.   2. Food habits—
Psychological aspects.   3. Obesity—Psychological aspects.
4. Reducing—Psychological aspects.   5. Self-help techniques.
I. Title.
RC552.C65A27   1993
616.85′26—dc20   93-24177
                                  CIP

Lexington Books
An Imprint of Macmillan, Inc.
866 Third Avenue, New York, N.Y. 10022

Maxwell Macmillan Canada, Inc.
1200 Eglinton Avenue East
Suite 200
Don Mills, Ontario M3C 3N1

Macmillan, Inc. is part of the Maxwell Communication
Group of Companies.

Printed in the United States of America

printing number
1   2   3   4   5   6   7   8   9   10

For my father and mentor,
Morris B. Abramson

Contents

Preface

This is not another book promising quick, effortless weight loss, nor is it an anti-diet book demonstrating the futility of all diets. This book is not based on a twelve-step program for controlling your addiction or disease. Weight loss, dieting, eating disorders, and body image are all related, but are not the main focus of this book. This book is about eating and how it is affected by emotions. It presents practical methods, based on the principles of cognitive behavioral therapy for controlling emotional eating. Although much of the discussion is directed towards readers who are overweight, it should also be of interest to people with eating disorders, as well as normal-weight, noneating-disordered individuals who sometimes find themselves using food to make themselves feel better. Thus the intended audience is a large group of people who want to understand, and possibly change, the relationship between eating and their emotions.

I am indebted to the many behavioral scientists who have done the work that forms the basis for much of this book. Dr. David Burns' writings on cognitive therapy and Dr. Russell Ganley's review of the research on emotional eating were especially influential. I also need to express gratitude to the authors of the studies I have cited. Without their work, this book would have been based entirely on clinical speculation. In addition I'm grateful for the opportunity to have worked with the people whose histories are briefly summarized in this book. Although details have been significantly altered to protect their privacy and, in some instances, features of two individuals have been combined to make one case study, all of the examples in this book are based on real people. I only hope that I have done them justice, and that my respect and caring for them is apparent.

Although I didn't always take their advice, I'd like to thank my friends and colleagues who read and commented on one or more chapters, gave me ideas, or were otherwise helpful: Marv Megibow, Ph.D., Alayne Ronnenberg, M.S., R.D., Tom Duncan, Ph.D., Diana Solar, Ph.D., and Alan Bernstein, M.B.A. Margaret Zusky and Sarah Zobel of Lexington Books were supportive, helpful, and fun to work with. Without Margaret's encouragement, I'd probably still be talking about writing this book some time in the future.

In some ways, writing this book became a family affair. In addition to accepting my long absences, they helped in several ways. My son, Jeremy, installed several software updates and then patiently explained to me what I needed to do to get them to work. My daughter, Annie, took the pictures and helped with some of the clerical chores. I'm especially grateful to my wife, Crystal, who listened to me obsess endlessly as I was writing and then served as the first "editor." Not only did she read every word, pencil in hand, she assumed a disproportionate share of the household responsibilities while I was exiled in my office. I'm lucky to have such a supportive family.

1

The Connection Between Emotions and Eating

Sandy, a twenty-seven-year-old client who weighed 170 pounds, had been making slow but steady progress in controlling her eating until she went to her aunt's funeral. The trip back home to Omaha stirred up feelings, and Sandy had been overeating since returning from her trip. Sally was Sandy's favorite aunt, and like Sandy's father and herself, Aunt Sally had been fat. Sandy explained their relationship to me: "When I was growing up, all I ever heard was how much I was like Dad and Aunt Sally. She was my dad's sister, and they were close. She was a connection with him that's gone. I miss her." Sandy started to cry.

Sandy's tears and her increased eating provide a vivid example of the relationship between emotions and eating. She told me that she had tried to cry when she was home alone but couldn't. She knew that she was emotionally upset but wasn't sure why. Usually she fought with her mother whenever she went to Omaha, but on this trip they didn't fight. Since there had been no conflict, Sandy saw no reason to be upset. Nevertheless, she realized that her overeating had started when she got the call about Aunt Sally's death.

Sandy's emotional distress and her eating started to make

more sense when we discussed her father's death from cancer. She explained:

> I was thirteen when Dad was brought back from the hospital to die at home. He had tubes running in him, and he required a lot of attention. My mother thought it would be best if he stayed in my bedroom. Every day from August to February I was with him as soon as I got home from school because I knew he was going to die. I wish I didn't remember how bad he looked. It makes me feel so sad.

When her father died, Sandy's mother instructed her not to cry. She should be relieved, she was told, that her father wasn't suffering anymore and had gone to heaven. The next day, the guidance counselor at school called her in for a talk, and Sandy, wanting to please the counselor, told him that she was fine. Although she had lost the only person who made her feel special, Sandy felt it was selfish to grieve.

It was not acceptable in Sandy's family to express feelings directly. On the other hand, the family encouraged using eating as a substitute for closeness and emotional support. With some help, Sandy identified the relationship between her eating and emotions:

> On the phone Aunt Sally always talked about food. Dad was like that before he died too. The only time I can remember much harmony in the family was at Christmas. The dining room and kitchen tables were full of food and desserts. It was the only time no one would bitch about how much I'd eat. It's just sad that it got mixed up because that's what I associate with comfort and happiness—the food, not the family and relatives.

The relationship between emotions and eating is clear in Sandy's case. The death of her aunt triggered more than the expected feelings of sadness and loss. Aunt Sally was a link to Sandy's father, and her death brought back the overwhelming feelings of helplessness that Sandy had experienced while watching her father die in her room. Sandy was able to see how her feelings had been suppressed and the connection between these feelings and her need to eat. With this understanding, Sandy could accept her sadness. Although remembering her father's death was still painful, she no longer had the internal turmoil that could only be calmed by eating. After the emotions were separated from eating, she was able to resume losing weight.

Most instances of emotional eating are not as dramatic as Sandy's. It doesn't take a death to trigger an eating binge. Can you recall times when your eating seemed to be uncontrolled, propelled by some force inside you? Maybe you didn't know why, but you did know that you felt bad, and you had to eat to feel better. Or perhaps you were not aware of how you felt but found yourself eating even when you weren't hungry.

Confusing Food with Feelings

The confusion of food with feelings—emotional eating—is very common. Even if you are one of the lucky few who isn't trying to lose weight, it is likely that some of your eating is tied to emotional states. Few of us view eating as purely nutritional replenishment. It is, after all, an activity that routinely takes up a large amount of time, and meals are milestones in our day. We do activities after dinner that would not be appropriate before breakfast. We have strong feelings about foods that we like or dislike. We socialize and celebrate with food. It is part of religious rituals. Virtually no one can be detached from or emotionally neutral about eating. This book is about the connections between emotions and eating.

Although the evidence linking eating to emotions is compelling, these findings should not be interpreted as demonstrating a link between eating and neurosis or any other type of psychopathology. Emotions are a part of the normal human experience. The fact that we refer to some types of psychopathology as an emotional disturbance or that emotions may seem to be exceptionally intense or uncontrolled in some mentally ill individuals does not imply that emotional states themselves are abnormal. Linking one normal human activity (eating) with another (emotion) does not create mental illness. Several studies of the mental health of overweight people have concluded that they are no more or no less abnormal than anyone else.[1]

Several popular programs nevertheless have conceptualized emotional eating as an illness or disease. Overeaters Anonymous (OA), for example, describes emotional eaters as "sick people" suffering from a compulsive "illness." They are "irresistibly driven toward the performance of some irrational action." The beliefs of OA are a modified version of the twelve steps of Alcoholic Anonymous. The first of the OA's twelve steps requires the emotional eater to acknowledge, "We admitted that we were powerless over food—that our lives had become unmanageable." This is rarely true. Most emotional eaters, even people with lengthy histories of anorexia or bulimia, are not entirely powerless over food. There may be episodes in which it seems that they have lost control of their eating, but there are other times in which they can exert control. The second half of the OA statement is even more fanciful. It is easy to see how alcohol, a potent drug with measurable effects on brain functioning, can ultimately lead to unmanageable lives. A brief visit to a detoxification center will provide many examples of lives made unmanageable by excessive drinking. Although some foods may have minor effects on brain function, eating a dozen doughnuts doesn't alter brain chemistry to the same extent as drinking a dozen bottles of beer. Only the most severely impaired anorexics or bulimics approximate the kind of chaos that frequently characterizes alcohol abusers. Most emotional eaters are quite capable of managing the responsibilities in their lives: they work or go to school, have relationships, behave responsibly, fulfill their obligations, and sometimes eat when emotionally aroused.

The second step in OA requires a belief that "a Power greater than ourselves could restore us to sanity." Subsequent steps refer to "a decision to turn our will and our lives over to the care of God," "a spiritual awakening," and so on. Certainly religious and spiritual beliefs are a source of strength for many people and can help motivate them to change, but it is not useful to think of emotional eating as a spiritual weakness, and it is not helpful to require that someone develop spiritual beliefs in order to change.

Going to meetings to receive support and encouragement from a group can be beneficial in making changes in behavior, but it is unfortunate that to get the support, you have to subscribe to the OA ideology, including the idea that you are powerless to control your "disease."[2] Emotional eating by itself is not a disease or an illness, and so having to endorse OA ideology can be counterproductive. One author, Wendy Kaminer, has described some of the problems with this approach: "Today's popular programs on recovery from various (and questionable) addictions actively discourage people from actually helping themselves. . . . Addiction is considered a disease of the will; believing in self-control is one of its symptoms."[3] Contrary to OA ideology, you can gain control of emotional eating. Once you can identify your emotional triggers and develop alternative behaviors, you will be less likely to experience the compulsion to eat or feel powerless over food.

The relationship between emotions and eating may seem obvious, but only recently has scientific evidence of the relationship been established. Until recently, therapists viewed eating as a method of reducing anxiety or stress that results from deeper emotional conflicts.[4] Anxiety is one of the emotions that may contribute to overeating but certainly not the only one. Depression, boredom, loneliness, and anger are a few of the others. Furthermore, the idea that the emotional state triggering eating is a consequence of a deep-seated conflict is probably untrue. Emotions resulting from the relatively trivial daily hassles of living are also capable of precipitating eating.

Understanding the relationship between emotions and eating and knowing how to use this understanding to gain control over eating is a recent development. This book is based primarily on scientific research dealing with eating, weight reduction, and emotions. In addition, I've added some of my own clinical experience and an occasional hunch. The purpose is to help you to understand your eating patterns and how they are linked to your emotions. This isn't always easy or painless. You will recognize, though, that your feelings, even the very strong ones, need not be terrifying or overwhelming. This book will help you to identify, accept, and experience these emotions without food.

A Confession

Before we go any further, I have a confession to make. Although I wore "husky"-sized clothes as a boy and fifteen years ago I was 20 pounds heavier, I am not particularly fat now. If you're an overweight female, you may doubt that a relatively slender male could understand your struggles with food. Before you give up on this book, let me reassure you. After working with almost a thousand overweight women and men and close to two hundred anorexics and bulimics, I have gained a sense of the emotions, thoughts, and behaviors that revolve around feeling fat. At times, it almost seems contagious. If I see a picture of myself or catch a glimpse in a mirror, invariably I'll notice my stomach hanging out farther than I think it should. I have to remind myself that I just had dinner, so my stomach is entitled to stick out; I'm *not* a fat slob. Other times I'll catch myself browsing through the refrigerator when I'm not hungry. Usually I can stop, identify the feelings that propelled me into the kitchen, and then decide if there is a better way of dealing with them.

My professional interest in emotions and eating started in graduate school. As I was getting ready to start my doctoral research, I read a series of ingenious studies conducted by Dr. Stanley Schachter, a psychologist, that suggested that for obese people, eating was triggered by external cues—the sight and smell of food, perhaps, or the time of day (dinner time, coffee break)—rather than internal hunger cues.[5] In one study, he demonstrated that increased anxiety did not cause mildly overweight college students to eat more food. Schachter was surprised by this finding since it was contrary to the widely held belief that eating served to reduce anxiety.[6] I was intrigued too. Although he had conducted a carefully controlled laboratory experiment, perhaps there was some mistake. I set out to prove that he was wrong by demonstrating what I thought was an obvious relationship between anxiety and eating. I didn't find it. My results showed that the overweight subjects who were anxious did not eat any more than overweight subjects who were calm.[7] I was disappointed but hooked. Since then most of my research and a good deal of my clinical work has revolved around issues of eating, emotions, weight, and body image.

Although I didn't find a relationship between eating and anxiety in my research, I frequently found it in my clinical work. Often a participant at one of the weight-control workshops I was leading would tell me about an eating binge the previous night. Although the specific circumstances varied, a common pattern became apparent. Most group members were successful using the behavioral techniques I suggested to change their eating habits; after several weeks, they were noticing weight losses and were feeling justifiably proud of their accomplishment. Then there was an emotional upset of some sort. It wasn't always a major trauma. More often, it was something as simple as frustration at work or an unpleasant telephone conversation with a difficult teenager. When this happened, the new habits were lost in the overwhelming urge to use food to make the bad feelings disappear. The feelings of accomplishment and the rewards of being thinner were swept aside in an emotionally charged moment. After eating a forbidden food, the participant would give up on herself, think something like, "Oh what the hell, I'm always going to be fat," and then continue eating until she felt full. Unfortunately, most of the behavioral weight loss programs of the 1970s did very little to deal with emotional eating.

On more than one occasion, a young woman would linger after a group meeting to raise an issue that she wasn't comfortable discussing in front of the whole group. Although the specifics varied, Ginger's problem was typical: "I know you talked about external cues that can trigger eating, but I've got a special problem. I binge. It doesn't make any difference if the TV is on, or what foods there are in the house. I'll binge on anything." This was my first introduction to what was then a little-known phenomenon, bulimia. Ginger, as is the case with many other bulimics, was testing the waters—hinting about her bulimia to see if it was safe to discuss her bingeing and purging. When she felt sufficiently comfortable, she told me the whole story. It was clear that emotions triggered almost all of her binges. Bulimics often report boredom, loneliness, or depression before bingeing and guilt, shame and sometimes relaxation after bingeing. Again, eating seemed to be intertwined with emotions.

It has been more than twenty-five years since I first read Dr.

Schachter's studies. We now have a more complete understanding of the relationship between eating and a whole range of emotions. In addition to the clinical evidence, more than eighty research studies link eating to emotions.[8] My goal here is to present most of this information to you in a way that will help you to recognize your unique patterns and, by following the guidelines I present, develop satisfying alternatives to emotional eating.

Dieting and the Causes of Obesity

Emotions play a contributing role in most instances of obesity and eating disorders, but they are usually not the only cause. Other variables such as heredity (it may be your parents' fault!), food choices, fat cell size and number, eating habits and activity or exercise patterns can be involved. After years of research on the cause of obesity, the one clear conclusion that has emerged is that obesity is multidetermined ——there are many possible contributing factors.[9] What this means is that you probably have wasted a lot of money, time, and painful effort trying methods that were ideally suited to someone else's weight problem. If you are overweight and your best friend is equally overweight, there may be different reasons for your respective weight problems and different solutions. Forget about swapping diets. Don't bother feeling guilty when one of your co-workers brags about how far she runs each day. What works for her may not be useful for you.

There is no good method for classifying different types of obesity and no simple method for you to unravel the mystery of your weight, but you probably have some ideas based on your experience.[10] When were you successful in reducing before? How did you do it? What was happening in your life that motivated you to make the effort that was needed? What happened to reverse your progress? It is likely that emotional eating was a significant factor in your weight gains and made it difficult to maintain weight loss even with a program that was initially successful for you.

Emotional Eating and Set Point

Recently several authors have argued that virtually all attempts to diet are doomed to failure.[11] According to this view, each of us has a genetically determined set point, a weight that is normal for us regardless of what the weight charts say or what the current standards of beauty dictate. Dieting may result in a temporary reduction, but the dieter will eventually return to the genetically programmed weight.[12] None of the adherents of the set-point theory believe that diets work, but some advocate exercising to lose weight. Others believe that we should learn to accept obesity as normal and stop pressuring fat people to be thin.

A fair amount of research supports the set-point theory, and it fits with our observations that some lucky people can control their weight more easily than most others. You probably know people who seem to be able to, or they eat what they want without gaining; and if they gain weight, they can lose it without much effort. Despite its appeal, however, set-point theory isn't very useful for most people trying to lose weight. Since there is no accurate method of measuring your set point, you have no way of knowing how much, if any, of your excess weight results from a high set point or how much of it is the result of foods you eat, a lack of exercise, emotional eating, or any of the other possible causes. Until someone develops a method to measure set point directly, you can only guess how much of a role it plays in determining your weight. And even if the set-point theory does prove to be valid (the final results aren't in yet) and you think that you are among those with a high set point, you still shouldn't give up. It is likely that emotional eating adds to almost all weight problems. One review of the studies in this area found that emotional eating was a characteristic of between 84 and 100 percent of obese women.[13] Although emotional eating was somewhat less likely for obese men, it seems safe to conclude that emotional eating is significant regardless of set point. For people with a high set point, controlling emotional eating may not be a complete solution to their weight problem, but it should be a substantial help.

Emotional Eating and the Decision to Diet

When you have controlled emotional eating, the decision to diet is an individual choice; only you can make it. Even though your doctor pressures you to lose weight, your spouse reminds you what not to eat, friends give you diets to try, and you have the feeling that you should lose weight, you still have the right to decide *not* to diet. There are dozens of perfectly rational reasons for making a decision not to diet. For example, if you believe that you have a high set point, you could reasonably conclude that dieting isn't helpful. Or if this is a particularly stressful time—you are going through a divorce, for example, or changing your job—you might decide to postpone dieting until your situation is more settled.

Let's assume, though, that now is a good time to start a diet. Why worry about emotional eating? Why not start another diet now? As long as there is a connection between emotions and eating, it is likely that an emotional upset will undo the effects of any diet. A review of seven recent studies of mildly to severely obese people trying to lose weight found that about 75 percent reported eating in response to negative emotions such as anger, depression, boredom, anxiety, and loneliness.[14] In other words, independent of whatever caused your excess weight, the chances are three in four that emotional eating will interfere with any diet or weight-loss program.

In Sandy's case, emotional eating both contributed to her obesity and disrupted her best efforts to lose weight. In fact, several predisposing factors made it very likely that she would be fat. The first was heredity. She was genetically programmed to be a large woman. She is 5 feet, 9 inches tall and has a large frame. No diet is going to decrease the size of her shoulders; she will never be petite. Furthermore, since her father and her father's sister were fat, it is likely that she inherited a predisposition to be fat. We cannot be sure since the gene or genes for obesity have not been identified, but it seems likely that her genetic makeup predisposes her to being fat.

Several psychological factors could have contributed to her obesity as well. One was repeated conflict with her mother over her weight. Although Sandy was only slightly overweight as an adolescent, her mother would find diets for her to try and frequently reminded her not to eat fattening foods. She would suggest that a large girl would look better wearing some styles or colors but not others. Sandy hated her mother's continual reminders but felt bad when she argued with her mother since Sandy accepted that the reminders were "for her own good." Many of the typical adolescent conflicts regarding control versus independence from parents tend to be expressed in arguments about eating and weight. It is also quite likely that the way Sandy was fed as an infant and young child contributed to her current problems with weight. In her family, sweets were used as a reward and an expression of love. Ice cream sundaes were the usual payoff for a good report card.

Emotional eating contributed to Sandy's obesity but did not by itself cause the problem. Nevertheless, emotional eating triggered by her aunt's death caused Sandy to give up a weight-control program that was having some success.

The negative consequences of emotional eating are greater than just missing another opportunity to reduce. Given our preoccupation with weight, a diet usually becomes a major focus of the dieter's life. Food shopping, preparation, and mealtime revolve around dieting, and it can become a focus of social interactions. Friends and family know that you are dieting. Your progress—or lack of it—is a frequent topic of conversation. If, after making some progress, an episode of emotional eating results in your giving up the diet, you may feel as if you have failed. And with the failure come self-recrimination, guilt, embarrassment, and depression—the same emotional states that make it more likely that you will fail at your next diet. You can get off the merry-go-round only when eating has been disengaged from emotions.

Since emotional eating will either disrupt a diet or, more likely, result in giving it up entirely, controlling emotional eating is a prerequisite for weight loss. *Ultimately no diet will work as long as you eat in response to emotions.*

This is not another diet book promising a new, effortless program that will produce quick weight loss. This is not a diet book at all. There are no menus or lists of forbidden foods. Rather than being about what you eat, this book is about why you eat. You will learn to identify your patterns of emotional eating, disengage the eating from the emotion, and, finally, develop effective strategies of experiencing the emotion, and doing whatever is necessary to become comfortable with it, or correct the situations that produce it. When emotions become separated from eating, then you will be ready to decide which, if any, method of reducing you want to try.

Are You an Emotional Eater?

Eating can be triggered by a single emotion or several. It can also be triggered by emotional confusion—a vague, generalized feeling of emotional distress. The relationship between an emotional state and eating is far from straightforward, however. The emotional state may set into motion a sequence of eating behaviors that may take place over a period of hours, or it may be immediately followed by a brief episode of eating lasting only a few minutes. For some individuals, a specific emotional state may be linked to a craving for a specific food, and only that food will satisfy the craving. For other people, an emotion may trigger a craving for a type of food, like salty snack foods or smooth, creamy foods. Any food from the category will work; you can substitute pretzels for potato chips. But much emotional eating is nonspecific; the emotion provokes an undifferentiated food craving, and any palatable food will do. This chapter outlines some of the patterns of emotional eating and provides you with guidelines for identifying your individual pattern.

Are you an emotional eater? The answer is likely to be yes. Aside from the obvious fact that you are reading this book, the reality is that almost everyone eats in response to emotional arousal, at least occasionally. Before attempting to reduce emotional eating, you need to learn more about it. How much of your eating is determined by emotions? What are the patterns that characterize your emotional eating? Do you eat in response to any emotional arousal, or are there one or two specific emotions that trigger eating? Are there certain people or locations or situations that make emotional eating more likely?

We will assess emotional eating in two ways. First, you will complete the Mood Eating Scale to get an overall measure of emotional eating. This objective measure of mood eating tendencies was originally developed for use with college students by Linda Jackson and Raymond C. Hawkins II.[1] Comparing your score to the norms for this measure will help to determine how much of a problem emotional eating is for you. Then you will monitor your emotional eating. Using the methods presented in this chapter, you will be able to start to identify specific relationships between emotions, situations, and eating. Several of the common patterns of emotional eating will be described and illustrated with case histories. Reading about other people's patterns of emotional eating may help you to identify your own habits.

Begin by completing the Mood Eating Scale (Table 2-1). To score it, first give each of your answers a numerical score. For each A, score 4, each B is 3, each C is 2, each D is 1, and each E is 0. Write in the score for each question next to the letter. After you have done this for all twenty items, go back to items 2, 4, 8, 9, 12, 14, and 18 and reverse the score for these seven items: a 4 becomes a 0, a 3 becomes a 1, a 2 stays the same, a 1 becomes a 3, and a 0 becomes a 4. For example, if you answered B on item 4 ("Eating something does not help soothe me when I'm feeling frustrated"), you would have scored this with a 3. Now reverse it, and give it a 1. The last step in scoring is to add up the numbers for the 20 items to get a total

TABLE 2-1

Mood Eating Scale

Instructions: Indicate how strongly you agree or disagree with each of the following statements by choosing the appropriate letter on the scale A, B, C, D, or E:

Strongly Agree				Strongly Disagree
A	B	C	D	E

For example, if you strongly agree with a statement, mark down choice A. If you strongly disagree, choose E. If you agree somewhat you might choose C.

1. Eating can make me feel somewhat relieved when I am overwhelmed with things to do.
2. When I am nervous, eating something will not help calm me down.
3. When someone important does something that clearly shows his or her dislike for me, I find myself eating after it happens.
4. Eating something does not help soothe me when I'm feeling frustrated.
5. When I am extremely happy, eating something seems to add to the good feeling.
6. If I eat a certain food and I feel very guilty about eating it, I continue to eat more of that food or other foods.
7. I find myself eating more than usual during periods of great stress (e.g., breaking up with a lover, final exam week, starting college or a new job, getting married).
8. If I was upset because of an argument I had with someone special to me, eating would not help soothe me.
9. I rarely find myself eating to pass the time when I bored.
10. When I feel inferior to someone, it makes me want to eat.
11. I seem to eat more than usual when I feel things are out of control.

T A B L E   2 - 1   (continued)

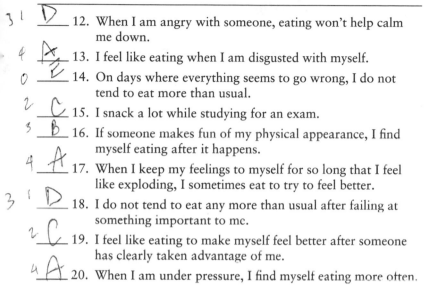

3 1 __D__ 12. When I am angry with someone, eating won't help calm me down.

4 __A__ 13. I feel like eating when I am disgusted with myself.

0 __E__ 14. On days where everything seems to go wrong, I do not tend to eat more than usual.

2 __C__ 15. I snack a lot while studying for an exam.

3 __B__ 16. If someone makes fun of my physical appearance, I find myself eating after it happens.

4 __A__ 17. When I keep my feelings to myself for so long that I feel like exploding, I sometimes eat to try to feel better.

3 1 __D__ 18. I do not tend to eat any more than usual after failing at something important to me.

2 __C__ 19. I feel like eating to make myself feel better after someone has clearly taken advantage of me.

4 __A__ 20. When I am under pressure, I find myself eating more often.

MOOD EATING SCORE _____

Source: J. L. Jackson and R. C. Hawkins, Stress related overeating among college students: Development of a Mood Eating Scale (unpublished manuscript, 1980). © Linda J. Jackson and Raymond Hawkins II, 1980.

Mood Eating Score. Write in your score in the space provided. As you work through the program presented in this book, you will probably want to take the scale again so that you will be able to compare it to your score today to see how much progress you have made.

The higher your score is, the more likely it is that you eat in response to emotions. For women in the original group given the test the average score was 34; for men, the average was 27. Check table 2-2 to see how your score compares with the norms for women or men. In the original study using this scale,

TABLE 2-2
Norms for the Mood Eating Scale

Women		Men	
Score	Percentile	Score	Percentile
19	16	15	16
34	50	27	50
49	84	39	84
64	98	51	98

emotional eating was more common among the women tested than the men. Higher scores were associated with anxious or restless moods and negative feelings about oneself while eating. Although not all dieters or overweight participants were high on emotional eating, very high scores were likely to be associated with being on a restrictive diet and having tendencies towards binge eating. It may be that strict dieting *increases* emotional eating, especially binge eating (In chapter 4, you will be able to evaluate the effects of your past dieting on your emotions.) But before we consider the causes of emotional eating, let's find out more about your habits and see if they are consistent with any of the typical patterns.

Identifying Your Patterns

Knowing when you are likely to be at the greatest risk for emotional eating is helpful information. To identify your unique patterns, keep track of emotional eating for the next week using the Emotional Eating Record (Table 2-3). You can make photocopies of the record, or devise your own form using 3 × 5 cards that you carry with you, to record instances of emotional eating when you are away from home. You don't have to record all your eating—only eating that seems related to your emotions or moods. How do you determine if it's re-

TABLE 2-3
Emotional Eating Record

Time	Location/People	Food/Amount	Emotion (or thought)
Date _____			
7–9:00	_____	_____	_____
9–10:00	_____	_____	_____
10–11:00	_____	_____	_____
11–12:00	_____	_____	_____
12–1:00	_____	_____	_____
1–2:00	_____	_____	_____
2–3:00	_____	_____	_____
3–4:00	_____	_____	_____
4–5:00	_____	_____	_____
5–6:00	_____	_____	_____
6–7:00	_____	_____	_____
7 8:00	_____	_____	_____
8–9:00	_____	_____	_____
9–10:00	_____	_____	_____
10–11:00	_____	_____	_____
11–12:00	_____	_____	_____
12–7:00	_____	_____	_____

lated? There is no completely objective method, so you have to decide for yourself if you are eating emotionally. For example, you can ask yourself, "Am I hungry?" "Is this a regular meal or a planned snack?" Although it is possible for emotional eating to occur in the context of a routine meal, it is far more likely when snacking or nibbling. If you are still not sure if the eating you have just finished was caused by emotions, write it down anyway on your Emotional Eating Record.

It is not necessary for you to be precise in writing every .ning you ate or to worry about counting calories. Right now, all that we are interested in is determining when your emotional eating is likely to occur and the circumstances that elicit it. After you have this information, you will be more effective in targeting your prevention and control strategies. But although the aim is not absolutely accurate records, it is important that you try to record each instance of emotional eating.

Keep your record keeping confidential. Since you may feel a little embarrassed about some of your emotional eating or you may not want to get "caught" if you have been "sneaking" food, you probably won't want to share your records with others even if they are trying to be helpful.

One final caution: At this point it's easy to tell yourself that you'll read through the book first and then go back and do the recording. The problem with this strategy is that you won't have the information you will need to implement some of the methods presented in future chapters. By reading the book, you'll learn about emotional eating, but you won't change anything unless you actually use the techniques, starting with self-monitoring. So continue reading, but start *now* to record your emotional eating.

Try to record your emotional eating as soon as it occurs so that the records will be accurate. The passage of time has a way of playing tricks with memory, especially when there might be embarrassment or self-consciousness about eating.

You are the only one who will see these records, so there is no reason to minimize or "forget" some of your emotional eating. Besides the temptation not to record emotional eating, the other difficulty is likely to be identifying the emotion in the last column. Frequently emotional states are confusing, and it is hard to come up with a single term that accurately describes what you are feeling. Keep in mind that emotions are not always pure experiences. Social psychologist Carol Tavris has suggested that, like grapes, emotions come in bunches.[2] You may write in two or more emotions for a single eating episode.

Sometimes the feeling itself might be confusing. You will learn how to identify emotions in chapter 6, but if you are having difficulty now, write in a question mark and then a note about your thoughts just before eating. Don't write in a food-related thought ("I wonder where I left the peanut butter?"); rather, try to recall what you were thinking just before the idea of food popped into your head. This will be helpful information later. For example, just before I started to write the last sentence, I was thinking about the classes I will teach next semester. Now, when I stop and focus on that thought, I recognize some internal signs of anxiety. I am anxious because I still haven't turned in all the materials that I need to have typed by next week, and I am dreading that I will have to turn away students who cannot be accommodated because of cuts to the university's budget. By directing my attention to a thought, I can identify an emotion that wasn't immediately obvious. In a similar manner, you will be able to play detective by using your thoughts to track down your feelings.

At the end of a week of recording, you should have some sense of the pattern of your emotional eating. If not, you may want to continue with your Emotional Eating Record for another week. If you forget to record your emotional eating, don't get discouraged or give up. Just start again on the next day. The record is still useful even with gaps.

After you have at least seven days of records, go back and look at the Time column. On a blank form, make tally marks next to each time period for each instance of emotional eating to determine when your emotional eating is most likely to occur. Next, review the Location/People column. Again, make a list of the different locations and any people who are with you. Tally the frequency of emotional eating at each site and with each person. Do the same with the foods recorded in column 3. Is there a favorite site for emotional eating? Are there favorite foods? (For the moment, ignore the emotions or thoughts recorded in column 4.) Have you noticed any patterns? Do some times or places or people keep reappearing? Do you have favorite foods to eat when you're emotionally aroused?

Now look at the last column. Do you find one or two emotions being repeated? This information suggests where you will have to focus your attention. Perhaps you find that you eat in response to almost any emotional arousal or that the column is full of question marks indicating that you are not sure what you were feeling. Even if no pattern of emotions is apparent or you are having difficulty identifying your emotional states, it is useful to know when and where you have the greatest risk for emotional eating.

Sneaky Snacking

Susan is a divorced forty-one-year-old mother of two who works as a claims processor in an insurance office. Her pattern of emotional eating, which I call sneaky snacking, is quite common:

> I never have problems in the morning. I'm so busy getting the kids ready for school and myself to work, I'm lucky if I get to gulp down my coffee. Sometimes I'll have some cold cereal or toast, but if I'm rushed I won't eat anything. At the office, I'll

have something during coffee breaks, and I go out to lunch with a couple of my friends, but this isn't emotional eating. I usually get home around 5:45 and rush to prepare dinner, but the emotional eating doesn't start until the dinner dishes have been cleared away. When I finally get to sit down and relax, the cravings begin. Sometimes it's better when I call a friend and talk on the phone for a while, but then when I hang up, I turn on the TV and start to snack. I find myself in the kitchen sneaking food. Sometimes it's cookies; other times I'm standing over the sink eating leftovers without using a plate. Even though the kids are in bed, I want to eat quickly and not leave any evidence so that I won't get caught. I know it's foolish. I guess I think if I do it quickly and don't make a mess, I'm not really eating. I don't know why I'm doing it, I'm not really hungry. But if I try to resist, I feel a craving that doesn't let up.

Susan's daily routine keeps her so busy that the emotions that trigger eating don't have the opportunity to surface. She generally likes her job and enjoys the opportunity to socialize with her co-workers. Taking care of her children, work, cooking, and all of the other daily chores fully occupy her conscious awareness. Only later in the day, when the pace slows, do her emotions emerge, followed by eating.

Susan's pattern is quite common. Although there is no research on the effect of time of day on the likelihood of emotional eating, clinical experience suggests that most emotional eating occurs during the mid to late afternoon or evening and late at night. One study of snacking by obese people in a controlled dormitory setting found that all of the subjects consumed most of their snacks after lunch, even though a variety of snacks were available all day. When the pace slows, on weekends and holidays, emotional eating may start in the afternoon, but it is rare in the morning. For the majority of emotional eaters, morning and early afternoon are "safe" times.

Using the eating record, Susan found that most of her emotional eating occurred between 7:00 and 11:00 P.M. in the kitchen. She also discovered that she ate mostly sweets—ice cream, cake, or cookies—and the eating seemed to be triggered by boredom, loneliness, or a vague feeling of unhappiness. Susan was curious about her eating, so she kept the record for a month. She noticed that two or three times a week, when she was feeling especially lonely, she would call her mother in the evening. Most of these conversations left her feeling dissatisfied. Her mother would chat about the events that had taken place in her life but rarely asked questions or expressed interest in what was happening with Susan. These one-sided conversations left Susan feeling more alone than before. Usually she started snacking as soon as she got off the telephone.

For Susan, like many other emotional eaters, identifying the pattern was all that she needed to curb emotional eating. When she recognized that she needed companionship and emotional support in the evenings and that her mother would not provide this for her, Susan was able to get it elsewhere. During the day, she enjoyed talking to Kathy and Terry, who worked in her office, but she never extended the friendship outside working hours. It wasn't too hard to call Kathy, another single mother, and arrange for the two of them to do something together.

Grazing

Susan's after-dinner emotional eating is quite common but not the only pattern. Grazing—intermittent emotional eating in several different locations throughout the day—is a less intense but equally troublesome pattern. Tom, a participant in a weight-control workshop I was conducting, provides a good example of this pattern.

Tom was a good-natured, forty-two-year-old certified public accountant with a busy practice. Although he had been athletic in college, he had started to develop a spread around the middle of his 6-foot, 2-inch frame. I learned later that the only reason Tom had signed up to take my workshop was that his wife had been after him to "do something" about his weight. Tom wasn't worried about his weight gain, but he figured that taking my workshop was the easiest way to pacify his wife.

As one of the assignments, Tom kept an Emotional Eating Record for two weeks. The Food/Amount column didn't show any strong preferences. Tom corroborated this. He was not very picky about the type of food he ate. Although he had a few favorites, if they weren't available, he would nibble on something else. For him, the act of eating seemed more important than the food that he ate.

Tom's record showed no particular pattern for time of day or location of eating. There were some locations where he could not eat (the night class he was taking, for example), but he would snack in any environment where it was okay to eat and food was available. Since his wife kept the refrigerator stocked and his secretary did the same for the office refrigerator, he had ample opportunity to snack. During the previous four or five years, he had gained 30 pounds.

When I reviewed his Emotional Eating Record with him, Tom indicated that he rarely felt any strong emotion. In the Emotion column, "boredom" was the most common entry. There were several question marks indicating that he wasn't sure what emotion he was feeling, but most of the column was blank. There were no strong feelings like anger or panic. Although I was skeptical about the lack of emotions associated with eating, I did not have the opportunity to explore this with Tom in the workshop. Later, it became apparent that beneath his placid exterior, Tom harbored strong feelings that he had not recognized. Several months later, I saw Tom, and he reported that he and his wife had been to a marriage counselor (at her insistence). During the sessions, Tom recognized that he was angry with his wife. With the counselor's help, he was able to verbalize his anger and work with his wife to correct many of the frustrations that both of them felt in the relationship. I asked him to try to record his emotional eating again and to give me a call in a week. He called exactly a week later to report proudly that there was very little emotional eating, and he had not experienced the boredom and frustration that he had reported at the workshop. The grazing decreased after he was able to recognize the angry feelings and develop a method for dealing with them.

Binge Eating

A third pattern of emotional eating is more dramatic and potentially more dangerous than Tom's grazing or Susan's sneaky snacking. Binge eating, identified by Albert Stunkard over thirty years ago, is now one of the criteria for a newly defined disorder appearing in the most recent version of the psychiatric diagnostic manual.[5] An eating binge is usually defined as a rapid consumption of a large amount of food in a short period of time. Binge eating is usually done in secret with feelings that the eating is out of control. Bingers feel guilty and disgusted with themselves and often have a sense that they will never be able to regain control over their eating.[6] Unlike bulimics, who binge eat and then purge by vomiting or using laxatives, most bingers try to control their weight by going on a strict diet or starving themselves. Inevitably, the strict dieting sets up the conditions for the next binge. (See chapter 4 for a discussion of how dieting is often self-defeating.) Since most binge eaters are ashamed of their eating, they tend to be secretive about their binges. Although we may never have an accurate estimate of the frequency of this pattern, it is apparently quite common. One study of four thousand women at colleges in Pennsylvania, Colorado, and California found that 42 percent identified themselves as bingers, while only 4.4 percent met the criteria for bulimia.[7] In the general population (males and females of all ages) binge eating was found in more than 6 percent of the people surveyed and about 30 percent of overweight people in weight-loss programs.[8]

If you are a binge eater, you have probably avoided keeping an Emotional Eating Record. If you have recorded your eating, you may have minimized or forgot to include your binges. For most binge eaters, writing down everything consumed during a binge would be too painful. Fortunately, for our purposes, it isn't necessary for you to have an accurate record of the food consumed during a binge. Our interest is in the emotions that trigger the binge, so all we need to know is that a binge took place and the emotions that were associated with it. If you tend to have eating binges, all you have to do is write in an abbreviation or symbol for the binge in the Food/Amount column and then describe your feelings in the Emotions column. You don't have to remind yourself of all the food you ate, and there won't be any record.

A thirty-three-old woman named Penny provides a good example of the potential hazards of binge eating. Penny was a college graduate who worked as a customer service representative for the local power company. She was married to Burt and had two young boys. Penny was a pretty, tall woman with a large frame. When she first came to my office, she was within 7 pounds of reaching her weight goal (140 pounds), but she wasn't happy. In a soft-spoken, hesitant manner she started to tell me about her binge eating:

> Even though I'm close to 140, I still feel insecure about the way I look. All I think about is what I eat and how bad I look. I ate

a bag of cookies yesterday and felt depressed. I had a real sense of failure; my goal was not to eat. When I eat, I can't stop with a reasonable amount of food. I only feel good when I'm not eating.

I didn't learn until later that Penny's goal was literally, not to eat anything. She had joined a commercial weight-loss program six months ago and was considered one of their star pupils because she had lost 99 pounds. She expected to reach her goal and keep the weight off for a year so that she could earn half of the fee back. Penny's weight loss, however, had little to do with the program. Typically she would weigh in and buy the prepackaged foods on Wednesday. Then she would start a series of eating binges that would continue through Friday. Her favorite binge foods were M&Ms and bridge mix (a combination of chocolate candies), but she would also binge on cookies, ice cream, or other sweet foods. All of her binges were secretive; her husband, doctor, friends, and co-workers had no idea that she was eating so much food. She felt like a total fraud when they complimented her on her dramatic weight loss. So how did she lose so much weight with so much eating?

Penny wasn't a bulimic.[9] She did not induce vomiting or use laxatives or diuretics, although on rare occasions she would eat so much, so quickly during a binge that she became sick and threw up. Her secret was that she would stop eating on Saturday morning. During her five-day fast, when the starvation became unbearable, she would allow herself a tablespoon of peanut butter, but otherwise she would not eat anything until after the weigh-in on Wednesday. Not only did she feel out of control and ashamed of the Thursday and Friday binges, but the rest of the week she continuously struggled to override the hunger pangs, lightheadedness, and weakness caused by starvation.

Penny's binge eating was limited by her schedule of Wednesday weigh-ins, but it became apparent that the whole cycle could be related to emotional eating. She found it difficult to discuss her eating without expressing several deeply felt emotional themes. Penny's husband, Burt, did not know about her binges and starvation diet. It was easy to keep the secret because he was not very interested or involved in her life. She resented that he spent more time with his friends than he did with her, and she was frustrated by her inability to get attention from him. Penny was not very assertive with Burt so she rarely told him that she was feeling neglected. Every few weeks, though, the frustration erupted into a major blow-up, with Penny yelling at Burt and threatening to leave. After each one of these episodes, Burt retreated even further, and Penny felt guilt for her outburst, and abandonment since Burt would avoid her for the next few days.

In therapy, Penny learned to be more assertive. She was able to talk openly with Burt, revealing her binges and starvation and her need for more closeness with him. Over several months they were able to resolve some of their differences and regain the intimacy they had earlier. With Burt's support, Penny stopped starving herself, and the binges occurred less often and were less severe. With a more normal eating pattern, she regained 15 pounds before her weight stabilized.

If you are a binge eater, it's unlikely that your eating habits are as disruptive as Penny's, yet you probably can relate to the awful feeling of being out of control while eating. Even if most binge eating is not so severe, the psychological effects of it are usually significant. Researchers at Kent State University had fifteen binge eaters, who averaged 3.9 binges each week, keep track of their emotions and physical states immediately after the binge and again one hour later. The most common emotions after bingeing were feeling fat (most were normal weight), being angry with oneself, and feeling tired, guilty, and stressed. They also reported having abdominal pain and headaches after binges. They did not have these negative emotions or physical symptoms after normal eating. If binge eating causes so much unpleasantness, why would anyone do it? The researchers think that "the act of binge eating temporarily distracts the individual from negative emotions."[10] Basically, binges are a more extreme form of emotional eating. In a related study, the same psychologists had binge eaters record their moods as soon as they had finished eating. Binge eaters, regardless of whether they were overweight, experienced more intense fluctuations in feelings of anxiety and depression when compared with nonbingers.[11] Binge eaters were more likely to experience anxiety and depression while eating, especially when they were binge eating.

Binge eating, grazing, and sneaky snacking are probably the most common but certainly not the only patterns of emotional eating. There are other variations that occur less frequently. For example, Dr. Stunkard identified a pattern of night eating that may be a more extreme form of sneaky snacking that develops in some obese individuals.[12] Typically night eaters have no appetite in the morning and rarely eat anything before dinner. After dinner, they experience a nonspecific anxiety that causes eating and increases as the evening goes on. Often they are agitated and can't sleep, staying up until 2:00 or 3:00 A.M. snacking. In other reported cases an obese person woke up several times each night feeling anxious and wasn't able to go back to sleep without eating.[13]

If, after keeping your Emotional Eating Record, you find that your emotional eating fits one of the patterns described, you may be able to control it easily. For many emotional eaters like Susan, awareness of the pattern makes control straightforward. On the other hand, you may find that although your emotional eating is entirely predictable—you

know where, when, and why an emotion will cause eating—
you still are struggling to control the eating. If this is the case,
you will have to work on dealing with the emotion and finding
satisfying means of coping without using food. Chapters 5
through 11 will show you how to do this. Even if you find that
your emotional eating does not fit neatly into one of the patterns or if it is a combination of two or more patterns, you can
still use the programs in these chapters to work on each instance of emotional eating. Now, while you continue to record
your emotional eating, let's look at some of the possible
causes.

3

Why Emotional Eating?

In this chapter, we will examine some of the possible factors contributing to your emotional eating. At best, however, we will be able to develop only reasonable guesses regarding the cause of emotional eating. Studies of these causes are just starting, so there are not many conclusive findings yet. Additionally, it is unlikely that there is a single cause for your emotional eating. You are a unique individual. What you do is determined by many variables—some of them biological, some relating to your culture, others going back to specific incidents in your childhood or behavior patterns in your family. No single finding will allow you to know exactly how a pattern of emotional eating developed. Still, if you examine some general principles, you should be able to get an idea of the factors that contribute to your unique pattern of emotional eating. Although the conclusions must be tentative, having a partial understanding of the origins will be useful in helping to control emotional eating.

Nutrition

First, let's look at the foods themselves, in terms of how they affect emotions. Your diet may contribute to emotional states, which then trigger additional eating.

Judith Wurtman, a nutritional researcher, offers evidence that for some people, specific emotions are a consequence of their diet. "Carbohydrate cravers" for example, experience irritability, agitation, or boredom and apathy as a result of lowered levels of serotonin in the brain. Serotonin is a chemical that serves as a neurotransmitter. It is found in the synapses—gaps, between nerve cells in the central nervous system—and is involved in the sequence of events that take place whenever the brain is processing information or controlling any of the body's functions. According to Dr. Wurtman, "When the brain is actively using serotonin, feelings of stress and tension are eased and the ability to concentrate is enhanced." [1] For most people, levels of serotonin in the brain tend to remain stable throughout the day. For a minority, serotonin levels drop in the afternoon, leading to feelings of agitation, irritability, or tension. Calmness and a sense of well-being can be restored by eating a snack rich in carbohydrates. For some people, then, some of their emotional eating can be attributed to biochemistry.

Although it is not clear why some people maintain a constant level of serotonin while others do not, it is clear what can be done to control the problem. To see if you are a carbohydrate craver, check your Emotional Eating Record to see if there is a pattern of mid-afternoon snacking. If it is almost a daily occurrence, look to see if the snacking is associated with anxiety, tension, or irritability. Although the exact words you used to describe your emotional state are not that important, it is important to note that this pattern is not usually associated with other emotions like depression and anger. Finally, are your mid-afternoon snacks sweet or starchy foods? If you answered "yes" to all of these questions, you may be a carbohydrate craver. There may be a physical cause for at least some of your emotional eating. If this is the case, a relatively simple change in diet should be able to prevent the problem. You can alter your diet to maintain adequate serotonin production. Dr. Wurtman suggests that you plan a light, low-fat snack like rice cakes or saltines in the afternoon. If you are not concerned with calories, an ounce of jelly beans or M&Ms works just as well, although carbohydrate cravers should stay away from pure chocolate. Chocolate is high in fat, which slows the digestive process; therefore it takes longer before the serotonin is produced.[2]

Even if you are not a carbohydrate craver, your choice of foods may still affect your emotions. Dr. Wurtman suggests that meals high in fat divert blood from the brain to the stomach and intestines for the lengthy process required to digest fat.[3] As a result, thinking becomes slower, and you start to feel lethargic or drowsy. Other possible mood-altering foods are sugar and caffeine. Psychologists at Texas A&M University put their subjects on a diet free of sugar and caffeine.[4] After their subjects' moods had stabilized, they added Kool-Aid made with either sugar or with Nutrasweet and capsules containing either caffeine or cellulose (which has no effect), and they related fluctuations in mood to the changes in diet. About half of the subjects experienced significant improvements in mood when they followed the sugar- and caffeine-free diet and then did worse when sugar and caffeine were restored to their diet. This group, which the researchers call dietary responders, showed feelings of fatigue, moodiness, nervousness, and depression when their diets included sugar and caffeine. Not all of the responders followed the same pattern. Although most responded slowly to the effects of sugar so that the deterioration in mood was not significant until the sixth day, one subject asked to stop drinking the Kool-Aid after a single day because she felt anxious and depressed. The researchers were not able to provide any guidelines for determining who was going to respond, nor could they predict the rate or exact emotional pattern of the response, so there is still no way of knowing if you are a sugar or caffeine responder without doing your own experiment. (In chapter 7 you will learn how to tell if you are a responder, and if you are, how to control your depressive moods by changing your diet.)

Other types of foods may affect mood too, but this area of research is new. We don't yet know how much of a role nutrition plays in emotions or why some people seem to be affected by their food choices. Even if you are a responder, it is likely that food choice is just part of your emotional eating. Psychological factors, perhaps dating back to your early childhood, are likely to play a role.

Childhood

It's almost a cliché to talk about experiences in infancy as affecting later eating patterns, especially emotional eating. Most parents have given some thought to issues like breast feeding versus bottle feeding and the best time to wean their children. Implicit in this interest is the idea that early feeding experiences have far-reaching consequences on later personality. The work of psychoanalytic theorists has filtered into mainstream culture through the writings of Dr. Spock and other authors, as well as countless articles in popular magazines.[5] Although the psychoanalytic approach reached the peak of its popularity during the 1950s, it remains quite influential, especially with therapists who work with obese and eating-disordered patients. For you to understand the origins of your own emotional eating, it might be helpful to consider some of the early experiences that psychoanalysts view as critical in the development of eating behaviors.

During the first year of life, infants learn about the world by using their mouth. Almost everything they touch automatically goes into it. During this time, the first love relationship that develops is between the infant and the mother, and much of their interaction revolves around feeding. Because of the physical contact, cuddling, and nurturing that occur while the child is being fed, an association develops between love and nurturance and eating. If development continues normally, the child's experiences expand, and these pleasant oral activities become part of a larger group of sensory experiences. Most adults still enjoy activities involving the mouth—eating, kissing, and talking—but usually there are other pleasures in life as well.

If the environment is less benign during the first year of life, the child may become orally fixated. Usually this happens when the child has been denied sufficient oral gratification—by premature weaning, for example—but fixation can also happen when the child has been overindulged. In either case, the child is unable to move on to develop other sources of gratification and as an adult relates to food as if it were the primary, or perhaps the only, source of emotional support. When this orally fixated adult is confronted with any emotional stress or even with the normal frustrations of daily life, he or she will use food to try to regain the security and comfort that was experienced as an infant being fed and cuddled.

This psychoanalytic explanation has a few possible shortcomings. It is not clear, for example, why some orally fixated people use food while others smoke, or drink, or talk excessively. Psychoanalytic theory doesn't explain how someone chooses a specific oral behavior. Another problem is that considering the whole range of oral behaviors—chewing gum, biting fingernails, being sexually aroused by breasts, and so on—it becomes clear that there are very few people who are not orally fixated. So if we're all orally fixated and the theory doesn't specify why some smoke, while others eat, the theory is not helpful in understanding emotional eating.

Hilde Bruch, however, a psychiatrist who has written extensively on obesity and eating disorders, has incorporated findings from child development research into the psychoanalytic framework and developed a more helpful explanation for emotional eating. Dr. Bruch suggests that when a mother is attentive to her infant's needs, she will offer food in response to signals (typically crying) that the child needs nourishment. This leads to the development of the sensation of hunger as a distinct idea that is different from other needs or sensations. But, she cautions:

> If, on the other hand, a mother's reaction is continuously inappropriate, be it neglectful, oversolicitous, inhibiting, or indiscriminately permissive, the outcome for the child will be perplexing confusion. When he is older he will not be able to discriminate between being hungry or sated or between nutritional need and some other discomfort or tension.[6]

Thus, food will be used for comfort when there is an emotional upset, though the individual is not physically hungry.

Even if emotional eating stems from experiences dating back to earliest childhood, it does not follow that lengthy psychoanalysis is necessary to change this behavior. After many years of clinical experience, Dr. Bruch concluded that psychoanalysis was not helpful in treating eating problems. I agree. Even if your emotional eating is a direct result of your early feeding experience, it is probably not necessary to try to relive or reconstruct these experiences. As we shall see, there are more direct approaches to changing this behavior.

Family

If nutritional deficits and early childhood were the only determinants we would expect that emotional eating would be consistent, day in and day out, regardless of time or place. Yet emotional eating does not occur in a vacuum. If you have been keeping your Emotional Eating Record for several weeks, you know that your emotional eating fluctuates. External forces, including your family and the larger society around you, play a significant role in your emotional eating.

Bernard Lyman, a psychologist, describes some patterns of family interaction that might lay the foundation for later emotional eating. Food can be used as a weapon, offensive or defensive, during family conflict. For example, when there are ongoing power struggles between parents and a child, demands such as "Eat your vegetables" or "You can't have dessert if your room isn't clean" can be a method for a parent to exert control over a child. Less obviously, children use food too: to resist parental control, to establish independence from their parents, and, possibly, to control them. According to Dr. Lyman,

> The parent says, "If you are good, you can have dessert," and the child thinks, "If you are good, I'll eat the food—if not, I won't." Unpleasant though it may be, this resistance to parental demands is not entirely undesirable. It helps the child's concept of self—the awareness that he or she is a separate person with needs, wishes, desires, and a separate will. It lessens the child's sense of dependence.[7]

In some situations, the battle for control goes beyond the development of independence. Dr. Bruch points out that a child's eating behaviors can provoke very strong emotional reactions in his or her parents.[8] Imagine that you are the parent of a nine-year-old obese girl. You are concerned about her weight and have gone to great lengths to encourage her to eat sensibly. You think you may be making some progress until you come home from work and find her finishing off a box of cookies. What do you feel? Anger? Disappointment? Frustration? Helpless? What are you going to do? Yell? Have another quiet talk about diet? Give up? Clearly the child's eating would provoke an emotional reaction from you. The most extreme example of eating being used as an emotional weapon in parent-child conflict occurs in many families with an anorexic daughter. As the anorexic starves herself to the point of ill health, the parents become increasingly panic stricken and desperate. Many therapists view anorexia as a last-ditch effort to exert some control by not eating.[9]

If a child learns that eating or not eating is her only source of power, the only way of expressing perfectly normal feelings like anger, or the only way that she may establish some independence from her parents, it is likely that she will be an emotional eater as an adult, especially in situations that elicit the same type of emotional response.

Jeanne's emotional eating probably results from this type of family conflict. Jeanne was a fifty-four-year-old married woman who was referred to me by her physician because she was still depressed despite trials on several antidepressant medications.

Jeanne had a very unhappy childhood. Her mother was an alcoholic who would run off with a man for months at a time, leaving Jeanne in the care of her grandmother, a cold, rejecting, controlling woman. Jeanne recalled that her grandmother frequently called her a "dirty thing" and told her that she'd "never amount to anything." The rejection was usually accompanied by criticism about whatever she was doing, along with suggestions for improvement.

When I first met her, Jeanne had been married to Tony, a successful farmer, for thirty years. She did not work outside the home and felt dependent upon, and controlled by, Tony. He was brought up in a traditional Mexican family where the husband was the boss. He did not understand his wife's depression or her physical complaints. Several years earlier, Jeanne had enrolled in a music class at the local community college but dropped out after several weeks of Tony's objections. He allowed her to volunteer at the local hospital but only if he approved of the times that she'd be gone from the home.

Although Jeanne did not seek therapy for eating problems (she was about 30 pounds over her ideal weight), one day she mentioned that she never got angry with Tony but ate "to teach him a lesson." He was unhappy with her weight and frequently nagged her about it. She had gained 14 pounds in the previous three months as she struggled to have some control in her life.

Eating served two functions: it was an indirect method of expressing anger, and it helped her to maintain some independence from Tony. The pattern probably had its roots in Jeanne's childhood interactions with her grandmother. As Jeanne became more assertive with Tony, the need for this type of emotional eating decreased. Apparently Tony was not able to adjust to a less-controlling type of relationship. A year after Jeanne had terminated therapy, she divorced Tony and lost about 20 pounds.

Occasionally the attempts of a parent to control the eating of a child reflect parental insecurities rather than a true battle of wills. This is particularly true for the idea of "wasting" food. Adults who have experienced deprivation as children may become upset when their own children don't eat everything put on their plate. Several years ago, I was conducting a weight-control workshop for nurses. An older nurse, with a European accent, took strong exception to my suggestion that it might be preferable to throw out small quantities of leftovers rather than to eat them. As a child during World War II, there had been times when she didn't have enough to eat. Although it was extremely unlikely that this would happen to her again, she could not accept the idea of throwing any food away.

Eating can play an important role in other types of parent-child interactions too. One fairly common pattern is to use foods as rewards. Getting an ice cream sundae to celebrate a good report card seems harmless enough, but it may represent a continuation of the association of love with feeding that the psychoanalysts described. Furthermore, the use of a specific food as a reward can result in that food's becoming better liked. Research has shown that when sweet and nonsweet snacks were given as rewards for good behavior, the snack food used as the reward became more desirable.[10] Thus using food as a reward may contribute to emotional eating in two ways: pairing food with love and approval makes it more likely that eating will become a substitute later, when love and approval are missing, and the type of food chosen for emotional eating may be a result of having been rewarded with that food during childhood. Check your Emotional Eating Record. Are there a few favorite foods that you routinely eat? When you are emotionally aroused and feel like eating, will anything do, or do you have a specific craving? Perhaps your favorite food may have been used as a reward when you were a child.

Cultural Rituals

British sociologist Anne Murcott describes eating habits as "a matter of culture, a product of codes of conduct and of the structure of social relationships."[11] Many important childhood events include social rituals involving sweet foods, and these rituals can set the stage for later emotional eating. For example, most children have birthday parties at which they are the center of attention; they receive cards and presents, and the highlight of this event is usually blowing out the candles on the birthday cake and eating it. Another childhood ritual involving sweets is Halloween. In addition to dressing up in costumes, much of the excitement comes from trick-or-treating and the consumption of prodigious quantities of candy. Perhaps the good feelings resulting from these childhood rituals combined with the family's use of sweets as rewards contributes to later emotional eating. One study[12] of college students found that during depressed moods, sweets were the most likely type of food to be eaten. Perhaps emotional eaters use sweet foods to bring back some of the positive feelings associated with childhood rituals.

In adulthood, certain foods have specific associations: popcorn suggests movies, bacon and eggs are for breakfast, and macaroni and cheese for dinner typically implies a tight budget. Some foods have meanings that elicit emotional responses, which in turn can trigger additional emotional eating. Everyone has favorite foods, and when they eat these foods they usually enjoy the experience. For dieters, though, favorite foods are "bad" and associated with a sense of failure. Eating even a few french fries or a small serving of ice cream provokes negative feelings ranging from guilt to intense self-loathing. I have had a few patients tell me that M&Ms, Oreo cookies, or potato chips are "bad" (or, in Weight Watchers terminology, "illegal"). The consumption of a single chip or cookie would result in misery, guilt, and self-recriminations. Paradoxically, in order to feel better, the dieter typically finishes the rest of the bag. If the favorite food had not been labeled as "bad" or "illegal" and had not been associated with dieting failure, it is likely that the additional eating would not have occurred.

One study of bulimics, binge-eaters, obese women, and normal-weight women found that meats, grains, and high-calorie foods were commonly thought of as "forbidden." Consumption of these foods often resulted in self-induced vomiting for bulimics and uncontrolled eating for bingers.[13]

Sexual Experience

The role that sexual abuse plays in the development of eating disorders is unclear. Many clinicians have reported that their bulimic, compulsive overeating, and anorexic patients were molested as children.[14] If sexual abuse is related to eating disorders, it might be a factor in the development of emotional eating.

One review of studies of the sexual aspects of eating disorders found no scientific evidence to suggest that sexual abuse plays a causal role in the development of eating disorders.[15] The authors of one research study that specifically addressed this issue suggest that both eating problems and a history of sexual abuse are common among women psychotherapy patients.[16] Since these patients are likely to discuss both issues with their therapists, it is not surprising that the therapists might assume there is a relationship between sexual abuse and eating when none exists.

Grace Lucido, a graduate student, conducted a study to attempt to clarify the relationship between childhood sexual experience and bulimia.[17] Women from psychology classes, bulimia support groups, and an inpatient treatment program were given questionnaires to measure bulimic behaviors and sexual events in childhood, defined as anything from "playing doctor" to sexual intercourse. She found no real difference between bulimics and nonbulimics and no differences between the groups in terms of the type of sexual activity (about 70 percent of both groups reported some childhood sexual experience). When she looked at the data more closely, she did find that bulimics reported significantly more sexual experiences with their fathers and brothers. She also found that the report of having had a negative emotional response—fear or shock—at the time of the sexual experience was strongly related to bulimic behaviors. Although the type of research design used in this study does not allow us to draw conclusions about causes, the findings seem to suggest that for women, childhood sexual experiences that cause negative emotions like fear or shock may be associated with bulimia later in life.

It is also possible that early sexual experience may be related to less severe eating problems.[18]

Perhaps by this point, you have some ideas about the causes of your emotional eating. Typically, emotional eaters can relate to one or two of the possible explanations, but there is no way to be certain. The good news is that it is not necessary to understand completely the reasons for emotional eating in order to change. Before we examine methods, let's look at how people usually try to control emotional eating. In the next chapter we will examine dieting, the most widely used method of changing eating patterns.

4

Dieting and Emotions

Are you on a diet right now? If you're not dieting, are you "watching your weight" or maybe just calorie conscious? If you are female and live in North America, it is improbable that you answered "no" to these questions. One study found that 82 percent of college women were either on diets or making some type of effort to keep their weight under control.[1] The *New York Times* reports that weight control is a $32 billion per year industry, although the number of dieters dropped to 48 million in 1991 from a high of 65 million in 1986. Nonetheless, sales of convenience diet foods and over-the-counter diet aids continue to grow.[2] Psychologists Janet Polivy and C. Peter Herman concluded that "it is now 'normal' for individuals in our society to express concern about their weight and to engage in fitful attempts to change it. A normal lifestyle now requires periodic exercise; normal eating now requires periodic dieting."[3] They view this "normal" and socially accepted pattern of dieting, however, as pathological.

Before you start worrying about your diet, let me reassure you: you don't have to make any decision about dieting right now. If you are on a diet and want to continue, feel free to do so. If you aren't dieting, it's probably best to wait until you've finished this book before deciding whether you want to start. Chapter 12 will give you some guidelines for making this decision.

Now we need to consider the effects that diets have on your emotional eating. To get a numerical measure of your dieting, complete the Restraint Scale (Table 4–1), which "is intended to identify people who, regardless of their actual weight, are dieters at least a good portion of the time."[4] To calculate your Restraint Score, give each item a 0, 1, 2, 3, or 4. If you choose the lowest or least frequent choice (the one on the left), score it 0; if you choose the response in the second column give it a 1; and so on. (Thus, if you circled "Usually" to question 1, give that item a score of 3.) When you have assigned a score to each of the ten items, add up the total to get your Restraint Score. Scores can range from 0 to 35. The authors of the scale consider women who score 16 or more and men who score 12 or more to be restrained eaters (or dieters); those scoring below these cutoffs are unrestrained (or nondieters).[5] After discussing the general relationship between dieting and emotional eating, we will come back to your Restraint Score.

Which Came First?

There is little doubt that a relationship exists between emotional eating and dieting. Less clear is the nature of that relationship. The typical dieter can describe the eating—much of it attributed to emotions—that led to the weight gain that they are now trying to undo with a diet. I was reminded of the widespread acceptance of this notion by a conversation I had after a talk that I gave at a meeting of mental health workers. In his introduction, the chairman of the group mentioned that I was writing a book on emotional eating. Although my talk was about anxiety disorders and I did not mention eating at all, later a woman told me about the emotional eating she had

TABLE 4-1

Restraint Scale

1. How often are you dieting? (circle one)
   Never   Rarely   Sometimes   Usually   Always
2. What is the maximum amount of weight (in pounds) you have
   ever lost within one month? (circle one)
   0–4   5–9   10–14   15–19   20+
3. What is your maximum weight gain within a week? (circle one)
   0–1   1.1–2   2.1–3   3.1–5   5.1+
4. In a typical week, how much does your weight fluctuate? (circle
   one)
   0–1   1.1–2   2.1–3   3.1–5   5.1+
5. Would a weight fluctuation of 5 pounds affect the way you live
   your life (circle one)
   Not at all   Slightly   Moderately   Very much
6. Do you eat sensibly in front of others and splurge alone (circle
   one)
   Never   Rarely   Often   Always
7. Do you give too much time and thought to food? (circle one)
   Never   Rarely   Often   Always
8. Do you have feelings of guilt after overeating? (circle one)
   Never   Rarely   Often   Always
9. How conscious are you of what you're eating (circle one)
   Not at all   Slightly   Moderately   Extremely
10. How many pounds over your desired weight were you at your
    maximum weight? (circle one)
    0–1   1–5   6–10   11–20   21

Restraint score _____

Source: J. Polivy, C. P. Herman and S. Warsh, Internal and external
components of emotionality in restrained and unrestrained eaters. *Journal of
Abnormal Psychology* 87 (1978): 497–504. © 1978 by the American
Psychological Association, reprinted by permission.

done recently and her plans to start a new diet to lose the
weight she had gained. Although this sequence seems consistent with the experiences of most dieters, recent research suggests that the sequence may be the opposite: emotional eating
may be a consequence of dieting. William Bennett and Joel

Gurin, authors of *The Dieter's Dilemma: Eating Less and Weighing More,* summarize this viewpoint:

> Reinterpreting fat people as chronic dieters puts the psychology of obesity in a whole new light. If dieting is the crucial variable, then the fat do not eat because they hurt inside; rather, they hurt because they are trying not to eat, to make their bodies conform to social norms. The struggle is constant, but lapses are inevitable, especially when emotions are taxed.[6]

Dieting and Depression

Interest in the emotional consequences of dieting was aroused by a study published in the *American Journal of Medicine* in 1957.[7] Albert Stunkard reported that nine of the twenty-five dieting patients he had been working with experienced emotional disturbances during their attempts to reduce. All nine went through an anxiety phase followed by depression. For some of the patients, the anxiety had been preceded by a period of mild elation, increased activity level, and feelings of well-being. This upbeat mood lasted for weeks or months but inevitably was followed by a period of anxiety and then a depression that might last for months. Although patients gave up their diets when the emotional problems started, the problems persisted long after the end of the diet. Since these were severely obese patients who were being treated in a hospital, Dr. Stunkard decided to do a follow-up study with a more representative sample of nonhospitalized dieters. Of the one hundred participants in an outpatient weight-reduction program, seventy-two had dieted before. More than half of them reported symptoms including nervousness, weakness, and irritability associated with their previous diets. Seventeen years later, Dr. Stunkard reviewed much of the research that had appeared since his original article and concluded that depression is frequently a consequence of dieting, especially if weight is lost rapidly.[8] He suggested that the high dropout rate reported by many diet programs may occur because dieters are trying to protect themselves from the negative emotions triggered by dieting. While some researchers haven't found depression after behavior weight-loss programs, Dr. Stunkard and his colleagues feel that the research methods used in these studies may not have been sensitive to the mood changes the participants experienced.[9]

What has your experience with dieting been like? If you've had some success, did you initially feel elated, only to become anxious, irritable, and, ultimately, depressed? If you've been through this sequence, what happened when you hit the anxious or depressed phase? You gave up on your diet, but did you resume "normal" eating, or did you find yourself overeating? In my experience, most disappointed dieters are depressed and angry with themselves for having "failed" one more time. Frequently they feel hopeless too. They tell themselves, "Since I'm never going to lose weight anyway, I might as well eat everything I want," and then use food to make themselves feel better. Sally is a good example.

Sally was an overweight, forty-six-year-old married mother of two, who worked as a teacher's aide in an elementary school. She complained to her physician about being tired all the time. The physician, who had known Sally for many years, told her, "You're not tired; you're depressed," and referred her to me. After talking with Sally for a few minutes and noting the sadness in her voice and on her face, I agreed with the assessment, yet Sally denied being depressed. Instead she focused on her shoulder pain, a recent bout with the flu, her tonsillitis several years ago, and a variety of other medical complaints. As she recounted the details of her recent medical history, Sally mentioned, with some shame, that she was eating "like a pig" and currently weighed 237 pounds, despite having attended a local weight-loss program. Clearly Sally blamed herself, especially her lack of willpower, for this failure. When I inquired about this experience, the nature of her depression became more apparent.

The weight-loss program had been highly recommended. During the first four weeks, she lost more than 20 pounds. She was thrilled! Her friends and co-workers noticed the difference and shared in the excitement. But after several weeks Sally's husband complained that she seemed crabby or tense. At about the same time, she missed one of the weekly weigh-in sessions. There was a plausible reason for missing the meeting, but in retrospect, it seemed that she was losing enthusiasm for the program. She became increasingly depressed and significantly increased her eating.

Dr. Stunkard speculates that the negative effects of dieting may have both psychological and biological components.[10] For Sally, many of the psychological components were easy to identify. Struggling with a diet brought back memories of being a "heavy" girl. Her sister was a cute, petite ballet dancer and their father's favorite. Sally, on the other hand, was a plump tomboy. Despite her good grades in school, Sally's father called her "a cow on roller skates." As a child, Sally had tried to diet to win her father's approval, but even when she lost some weight, she never could successfully gain his love and approval. As an adult, her marriage to Ted repeated many of the same themes. Ted frequently nagged her about her weight, but when she made some progress in reducing, Ted would still be dissatisfied.

From a psychological point of view, there was a predictable pattern to Sally's weight-loss efforts. She would make a significant effort and feel euphoric when she saw some results. As it became apparent that the weight loss would not have the desired effects—her father or her husband would still withhold love—she became irritable and then depressed. When depressed, she would turn to food for comfort and solace, regaining the weight she had lost plus a few additional pounds. The psychological pattern seems clear-cut. But there may be something happening biologically that is equally important. We'll come back to Sally to see how the internal physiological processes that maintain her set point could be responsible for her dieting—emotional eating pattern.

Diets and Set Point

As you will recall from chapter 1, set-point theory holds that there is an inherited set point, or ideal weight, that is biologically right for you, regardless of how you feel about it, what the weight charts say, or what current notions of beauty dictate. Richard Keesey, an experimental psychologist, compares set point to other mechanisms that the body uses to regulate itself.[11] For example, even if you traveled from a hot equatorial desert to frigid Antarctica, your internal body temperature would remain the same. Whatever happens in the environment, your body adjusts its internal workings to maintain a stable temperature. According to set-point theory, the same is true for weight: regardless of how you diet, the physiological processes that regulate weight will bring you back to your set point.

If you are one of the few who, by virtue of exceptional "willpower," could succeed in temporarily overriding your set point, your body will be in a state of semistarvation. According to set-point theory, this is true even if you still are pounds away from your goal weight. It is possible, for example, that you could be 20 pounds above your ideal weight on the charts and still be below your set point. Research has shown that people who are below their set point, whether they started out at "normal weight" or "overweight," will experience considerable psychological distress until they return to their set point. During World War II, Ancel Keys studied thirty-six conscientious objectors who volunteered to participate in a study of semistarvation. After several months on a diet that provided about half of their usual caloric intake, depressed mood was common, and they were irritable, apathetic, and quarrelsome. The psychological problems did *not* go away when they were finally allowed to eat as much as they wanted. Despite the huge quantities of food that they ate, it was only after the volunteers had regained the weight, or, in other words, returned to their set point, that they felt better.[12]

If we look at Sally's experiences now in terms of set point, it may be that her childhood experiences with a rejecting father and the current conflicts with her husband may be only part of the problem. It is possible that, having dieted herself below her set point, it was biologically inevitable that she would experience unpleasant emotions and give up on her diet. Once she stopped dieting, she would overeat but wouldn't feel better until she had gained enough to get back to her set point.

Perhaps you are getting a little impatient. Which view is correct? In all likelihood, both are, but until there is a method for measuring set point, we won't know for sure. Fortunately, we can use the Restraint Score as an indicator that will provide an approximate measure of both the biological and psychological effects of dieting.

Restraint and Hyperemotionality

Considerable evidence has accumulated on the undesirable consequences of dietary restraint. Research suggests that a high level of restraint is associated with increased emotional responsiveness, as well as a greater likelihood of losing control over eating. Keeping your own Restraint Score in mind, let's look at the effects that dieting has on your emotions first, and then see what happens when you are dieting, you experience emotional arousal, and food is nearby.

Several studies, including one that I conducted, have reported that obese people are more easily emotionally aroused than normal-weight people in the same situation.[13] In most of these studies, some kind of stressor was presented to obese and normal-weight subjects, and usually the obese subjects had a stronger or more intense emotional response. It has been suggested that given the social pressure to lose weight, most obese people are always dieting or at least watching their weight. Polivy and Herman view the hyperemotionality of the obese as a consequence of dieting rather than the result of obesity itself:

> In our view, however, hyperemotionality in dieters (and obese persons) is itself seen as a consequence of dieting; were an individual to forgo the attempt at weight suppression, such emotional over responsiveness would not be evident. Dieting, we argue, is a stressor, a source of frustration and a drain on one's resources to cope with the (emotional) demands that one encounters. Hyperemotionality, in turn, may simply reflect an emotional instability exacerbated by stress.[14]

When you are on a diet, are you touchy? Do you cry more easily or feel sad much of the time? Or perhaps you are tense, fearful, and generally uptight. It's not surprising that most people hate to diet. You are deprived of some of your favorite foods and may have more than your share of emotional upsets.

Dieting can make you more emotional than usual. Sally became crabby and tense. What happens when you are on a diet and emotionally aroused, *and* there is food nearby? The results of several studies suggest that fear and depression—or almost any other negative emotion—may make you abandon the diet and overeat.

Restraint and Fear

In a recent study, psychologists at the Chicago Medical School gave sixty college women the Restraint Scale and then had them view a twenty-minute excerpt from either a travel film about Australia or scenes from the movie *Halloween* in which the characters were being stalked by a killer. All subjects were given a bag of buttered popcorn to eat during the movie. The women who had high restraint scores and saw the frightening film ate more popcorn than women who were equally high on restraint but saw the travelogue. Women who scored lower on restraint ate about the same amount regardless of which film they saw. The findings suggest that a fearful situation, even a scary movie, can trigger overeating among dieters.[15] Similar results were reported in an English study of three groups of overweight women. Women in a diet group scored higher on a measure of restraint as the treatment progressed. Women in a discussion group and in an exercise (but no diet) group had lower restraint scores. When they saw a frightening film (this time it was *The Shining*), the dieters ate three times as much candy and nuts as the women in the other groups.[16]

Now check your Restraint Score. If it is above the cutoff score (16 for female, 12 for males), you are at greater risk for emotional eating triggered by fear. If you are going to continue to restrain your eating, you will need to develop techniques for dealing with fearful or anxiety-producing situations without eating. Chapter 8 should be helpful in this regard. In the interim, it should be helpful to know that you are at greater risk for unplanned eating when you are afraid or anxious. If you should overeat, at least you won't have to punish yourself. Instead of blaming yourself for a lack of willpower or some other vague character deficiency, you will be able to recognize the unplanned eating episode for what it was and go back to your diet.

Restraint and Depression

Fear isn't the only emotion that can trigger eating in dieters. In one of the earliest studies of restraint, Polivy and Herman showed a complex relationship between restraint, depression, and weight. They studied twelve normal-weight, clinically depressed patients at a hospital psychiatry unit and, using the Restraint Scale, found that the restrained patients had gained more than 6 pounds since becoming depressed. They think that the effort required to maintain a diet is disrupted by emotional states. A dieter who becomes depressed abandons the diet and eventually gains weight. On the other hand, for unrestrained eaters who are free to eat as much as they would like, depression seems to decrease appetite.[17]

Two related studies show that just about any unpleasant emotion can produce overeating in dieters. The first was a laboratory study in which normal-weight college women were given a phony "culture-free intelligence test" consisting of either unsolvable or solvable problems. Subjects who took the unsolvable test thought that they had done poorly and reported significant increases in depressed mood, hostility, and anxiety. They were then asked to taste and rate three types of crackers. They could eat as many crackers as they wanted while making the ratings. Dieters who thought they did poorly on the test ate more crackers than dieters who thought they did well.[18] The second study was conducted in a more natural environment. Thirteen English women dieters were asked to record everything they ate for one week and to make hourly ratings of their moods using rating scales that were provided. The researchers found that ratings of depression, anxiety, loneliness, and boredom were significantly higher before episodes of overeating.[19] Again, the results suggest that dieters who experience an unpleasant emotion are likely to eat more.

Taken together, these studies explain why dieting is so difficult. Even if we ignore the physical effects suggested by set-point theory, diets can produce several unpleasant psychological consequences. When you diet, you become more emotional, and when you experience a negative emotion and food is nearby, you are more likely to eat. No one ever told you about this when you started a diet! Usually diets or weight-loss programs are presented as being miraculous, or at least effortless. In the before and after advertisements, the smiling, successful dieter never says that she is now hyperemotional and the smallest upset sends her running to the refrigerator. The ads forget to mention that dieting may be a self-defeating enterprise—an unfortunate omission considering all the time, money, and effort that go into dieting. The shame, guilt, and self-recriminations after a dieting failure are even more unfortunate. When you gave up on your last diet, how did you feel? What did you say to yourself? Were you harsh, putting yourself down? Sally described herself as "eating like a pig" and viewed her situations as hopeless. She was angry with herself, disappointed, and ashamed.

Sally's shame is quite common. Kinsey, surveying sexual practices of American women, found that they were more embarrassed when asked about their weight than when asked about masturbation or homosexuality.[20] When I presented the information described in this chapter to Sally, she became more self-accepting. She recognized that some emotional eating is inevitable while dieting, and she learned coping skills to manage many of the emotional upsets that could trigger eating.

In the past five years, how many diets have you been on? How many worked? Can you recall why you went off your diet? One study of dieters in a medical center weight-loss program found that 49.5 percent of the relapses occurred while the dieter was experiencing a negative emotion—most commonly anxiety, followed by feelings of depression or anger.[21] Can you relate at least some of your past dieting failures to negative emotions and understand why they happened? I'm not suggesting that you give up dieting (although that is an option to consider later). Rather, if you see the role that negative emotions play in dieting failures and you can understand how dieting contributes to increased emotional arousal, you don't have to be so hard on yourself. You don't have to feel guilt or shame; you can relax. You're not hopeless; you're not a fat pig or even a cow on roller skates.

5

Eating and Self-Nurturance

How do you like yourself when you're on a diet? The act of dieting expresses a dissatisfaction with your body: it's too big, too fat, too flabby, or too something else that is unacceptable. If it was okay, why would you go through the physical and psychological discomfort of the typical diet?

The body that you don't like is *you*—not some alien structure superimposed on the real you. If there is no way of separating your body from the rest of you, how can you hate the most obvious, tangible aspect of yourself and still like who you are? The obvious but frequently overlooked truth is that it is hard to like yourself when you are dieting:

> One woman said to me: "Little by little I began to be aware that the pounds I was trying to 'melt away' were my own flesh. Would you believe it? It never occurred to me before. Those 'ugly pounds' which filled me with so much hatred were my body.[1]

Any dieter asked to list her goals for the next year in the order of their importance will put losing weight at the top—even if she is an energetic woman with a variety of interests. Graduating from college, getting a better job, learning to speak Spanish, or improving one's backhand will be second ary. The problem arises when weight isn't lost or is regained after an all-too-brief loss. The unfortunate truth, in fact, based on the best evidence we have, suggests that permanent weight loss is rarely accomplished. The results of hundreds of studies of the outcome of dieting have been summarized by A. J. Stunkard: "Most obese persons will not remain in treatment. Of those that remain in treatment, most will not lose weight, and of those who do lose weight, most will regain it."[2] If you are a dieter, how are you going to feel about yourself when, year after year, you fail to accomplish your most important goal?

Many dieters see their self-hatred as desirable. They think that they deserve all the put-downs, which they think will spur them on to more fervent adherence to their diet. They would argue, "I'm too fat. How can I like myself like this? Besides, if I like myself like this, I won't have the commitment to stick to my diet. I'd become complacent and stay fat like this for the rest of my life." This is one of the most unfortunate, self-defeating mistakes that a dieter can make.

If you are dieting and not feeing very good about yourself, you will tend to see yourself as undeserving and unworthy. Only after you have succeeded in losing weight will you deserve any of life's pleasures. How many times have you told yourself that you could not go on a trip or buy yourself a new outfit until you had lost 10 (or more) pounds? One patient told me she wasn't going to her high school reunion (four months in the future) unless she lost 15 pounds. Another patient wouldn't ride a bicycle or go dancing, and a third wouldn't buy any new clothes until she lost weight. Dieters usually end up cutting themselves off from pleasurable activities. Psychologists Susanne Doell and Raymond Hawkins found that overweight students in a weight-control program reported less enjoyment of pleasant activities in comparison to normal-weight college students. The psychologists suggest that this is unfortunate since the availability of pleasant activities may serve to "inoculate" emotional eaters from eating when they are stressed. On the basis of their clinical work at the University of Texas Psychological Weight Control Program, they conclude that clients who substitute an enjoyable activity for emotional eating report improved mood, increased motivation, and less likelihood of relapse after weight loss.[3] Being good to yourself and allowing yourself to have some fun may decrease emotional eating and make diets more successful.

Allowing yourself to have fun may be just one example of being good to yourself, or nurturing yourself. Researchers at Yale have studied styles of self-nurturance as related to disordered eating. They define self-nurturance as "an attitude directed toward the self that is self-comforting, accepting, and supportive. Central to this self-nurturance attitude is the ability to derive pleasure from positive experiences and to cope effectively with negative ones."[4]

If you are a dieter, you are not likely to be self-comforting, accepting, or supportive unless your diet has been going well for at least a week. If your diet hasn't been going well but you have a positive experience unrelated to your diet, that experience will be minimized or ignored—for example, your boss pays you a compliment, but you don't feel any better because you still haven't lost any weight.

Why should a lack of self-nurturance contribute to emotional eating? Janet Polivy and Peter Herman suggest that some dieters "have few ways to feel good or be nice to themselves other than by eating treats, often as not forbidden fruits of some kind."[5] Writer Kim Chernin describes her own experience using food for self-nurturance: "What I wanted from food was companionship, comfort, reassurance, a sense of warmth and well-being that was hard for me to find in my own life, even in my own home."[6]

Success, fame, and fortune are not defenses against emotional eating. Seven months after Naomi Judd left the mother-daughter country music duo, the Judds, daughter Wynonna Judd described her use of food for self-nurturance: "Food is such an emotional thing. When I'm feeling like I really want somebody to hold me like Mom used to do, rubbing my feet or patting me on the leg, I'm lonely and want to eat all the foods my mom gave me when I was a child."[7]

A lack of fun, or pleasure, or good feelings create a significant void. There usually is a nagging sense that something is missing, accompanied by frequent, sometimes frantic, efforts to fill the void with food. Psychiatrist Gerald Russell describes this feeling as "empty aloneness."[8] Most often these experiences are not consciously identified but are nonetheless powerful determinants of behavior. When good feelings don't flow from the activities and relationships of daily life, the deprived individual often tries to provide these feelings. Eating is probably one of the easiest methods to provide the pleasant feelings that other activities in daily life don't offer: it is easy; it is almost always readily available; it doesn't require the approval or help of anyone else; and, especially with snack foods, no special equipment or involved preparation is required. In other words, you can have what you want when you want it! Viewed from this perspective, eating is probably the most efficient, cost-effective method for nurturing yourself. The obvious consequence of using food for self-nurturance, however, is weight gain. Less obvious but equally important consequences include depression, self-recrimination following the emotional eating, and missed opportunity to find other pleasurable activities. Using food for self-nurturance makes it easy to postpone doing whatever it would take to find more satisfying ways of nurturing yourself.

Terry, a twenty-three-year-old single woman, provides a good example of someone who had few pleasurable activities in her life and instead used eating for self-nurturance. Coming to see me was Terry's parents' idea. Her father was a prominent dentist, and her mother, who accompanied Terry to her first appointment, was an elementary school teacher. Both were concerned: Terry's weight had increased from 150 pounds three years earlier to 230 pounds. Since Terry had not had any success with commercial weight-loss programs, her parents brought her to me to "get at the psychological roots of the problem." Like so many other times in the past, Terry dutifully complied with her parents' wishes.

She was a pretty young woman, impeccably dressed and well-mannered. Although she obviously had misgivings about being in a psychologist's office, Terry was gracious in responding to my questions:

> After I dropped out of college, I got a job as a nurse's aide in a convalescent hospital. My mother doesn't like it; she says only white trash will work at convalescent hospitals. My mother used to have all these expectations for me and tried to push me to do things. I guess now she knows she can't push. I used to be perfect when I was in high school. I had straight A's, was in student government, I hung out with the popular kids, I even had a boyfriend. My older sister, Bridget, was perfect too. She was the homecoming queen and a cheerleader, but she wasn't good enough either. The family was always in an uproar. Bridget was fighting with my mother, but I was the good little girl who would try to keep the peace. My dad used to tell me that I was so dependable. Boy, was he surprised when I dropped out of college.

Terry described a tightly controlled family environment dominated by her mother, who was intent on presenting an ideal image of their family life to the outside world. Despite his professional prominence, her father was ineffectual within the family. His contributions usually were little more than half-hearted endorsements of his wife's view of whatever was being discussed. In order to escape domination by her mother, Terry dropped out of college, moved out of their home, and found a job, but she wasn't able to make a complete break with her parents. She didn't have a car, so she would have to go back home to borrow theirs. Or she would frequently spend too much money and have to ask her parents for a loan. As a result, Terry was frequently at her parents' mercy. Whenever she needed anything from them, she would get it but only after listening politely to a lecture about her mistakes and how she had embarrassed and disappointed her parents.

Terry's description of her current situation sounded bleak. She lived in a small apartment alone. She did not feel comfortable socializing with her co-workers (the "white trash"), but most of her high school friends had moved on, either marrying or going off to college. Her only social outlets were the monthly meeting of a young women's social club and a male friend who was preparing to become a Catholic priest.

After getting to know Terry and establishing rapport and trust with her, I asked her to keep an Emotional Eating Record. Initially she resisted, but after being reassured, she consented to try it for a week. She kept the record for five of the seven days.

After two days on her best behavior, Terry's record on the third day showed six brownies with ice cream at 7:00 P.M. while feeling depressed. The next night at about the same time, she ate two tuna sandwiches, three helpings of potato salad, a handful of potato chips, two brownies, a piece of chocolate cake, and a piece of carrot cake while feeling relaxed and content. This was a daily pattern. Terry was a binge eater, although the binges were not associated with a single emotion. Terry used food to nurture herself. With some embarrassment, Terry told me that her binges were the high point of her day.

She looked forward to them. There were very few pleasurable activities in her life; there wasn't much companionship, comfort, or reassurance from others; and there was little that Terry did to be nice to herself other than eating.

How Do You Nurture Yourself?

Do you use food to make up for a specific loss, or does food substitute for a whole variety of empty places in your life? Check your Emotional Eating Record. You may find that when it was hard to identify an emotion, the eating may have been prompted by a need to nurture yourself accompanied by vague feelings of unease. Other times, there were probably more definable emotions like depression, anger, or anxiety. In either case, your task now is to develop methods for nurturing yourself without food. It will help to divide the task into two parts: developing self-nurturing behaviors and developing self-nurturing attitudes.

Self-Nurturing Behaviors

What do you like to do? What do you enjoy? For a moment think about the kinds of activities that give you pleasure. Exclude skiing trips to Vail or Caribbean cruises, and focus on more ordinary (and less expensive) pleasures—those that aren't too expensive and can be done daily or at least fairly frequently. Include activities that are simple pleasures. We are not looking for "peak experiences" or especially memorable events in your life, but rather routine occurrences that bring you some enjoyment. It does not make any difference if they are activities that you do by yourself or with other people so long as they can be done frequently and easily, without a lot of prior planning. On the lines that follow, make a list of as many of these activities as you can think of.

_____   _____

_____   _____

_____   _____

_____   _____

_____   _____

_____   _____

If you are having a hard time with your list, consider the kind of things you would like to do but don't allow yourself because you "don't have the time" or you don't think you have done enough to have earned it. For example:

plant a vegetable garden	get a massage
go to church or synagogue	volunteer at a hospital
sing in a choir	ride a different bus
watch a sunrise	paint your room
ride a bike	attend a play
take a bubble bath	call a friend on the telephone
take a drive in the country	take music lessons
take a walk	collect baseball cards
learn a new computer program	manicure your nails
browse in a bookstore	sit quietly doing nothing
make something out of wood	sew, knit, or crochet something
try a new hair style	play with a pet
organize a desk or file	try a new cologne or perfume
keep a diary	arrange flowers
browse in an antique store	dance to loud music
lie in the sun	throw a snowball at something

There are two steps to developing self-nurturing activities. First, identify the activities that appeal to you. In the next few days, think about what you would like to do, and see if you can add to your list. The second, and probably more difficult, step is to give yourself permission to do the activity even when you think that you don't have enough time, money, skill, or talent to do it. There will always be a reason *not* to do something, but nurturing yourself is important enough to overcome these hesitations.

Self-Nurturing Attitudes

Developing a self-nurturing attitude may be more difficult, especially if you have been dieting for years. The first step is to forgive yourself for your failures at dieting. I'm not suggesting that you accept your current weight or give up dieting (you'll make an informed decision about this after reading chapter 12)—only that you make peace with your previous unsuccessful attempts to diet.

It may help to recall some of your childhood aspirations. Did you want to be a cowboy, ballerina, movie star, or professional basketball player? What happened? Perhaps your goal was a little unrealistic. When you found out what cowboys actually do all day, you decided that you probably would prefer a different line of work. Or maybe you had physical limitations—you couldn't grow tall enough to be a basketball player or professional model. Whatever the reason, by now you have forgiven yourself for not having fulfilled your childhood dream. Do the same thing for your earlier weight-loss goals. Can you accept that your goals might have been a little unrealistic or that there might be physical limitations on the amount you were able to lose? There is no shame in not being a cowboy, nor is there in failing to fit into a size 11.

Without the continuous self-recriminations for dieting failures, it becomes possible for you to recognize your good qualities. When you evaluate your accomplishments without worrying about failed diets, you will find at least a few things you can be pleased about. You will find that you are a worthwhile individual. You can start to like yourself and nurture yourself.

Perhaps you have forgotten your good qualities. Even if you are not a dieter, you may have been taught that it is conceited to discuss, or even think about, your strong points. To develop a self-nurturing attitude, it is not necessary to brag about yourself but, rather, to make an impartial and objective assessment of your strengths. It will probably help if you pretend that you are someone else doing a background investigation of you. What would this impartial investigator find? Start with your job. What skills do you have? Do you type, draw blood, write programs, edit, garden, or teach well? How about your personal attributes? Are you friendly, trustworthy, or easy to talk to? Do you have a good sense of humor? Are you good with children? Next consider your hobbies and interests. Can you play a musical instrument, take good photos? Are you knowledgeable about baseball statistics or fashion design? Are you a good homemaker (yes, being a good cook counts!)? Can you organize things? Are you a good parent?

In all likelihood, you don't recognize your strengths, skills, positive attributes, and qualities. You may take them for granted, and when someone else appreciates something that you've done, you tend to dismiss or minimize it. Now be honest: when you read through the list in the previous paragraph and found something that applied to you, did you tell yourself, "Anybody could do that? It's no big deal"? It will be hard to develop a self-nurturing attitude if you cannot let yourself take pride in your successes.

On the lines that follow, list ten attributes or skills that you have. Remember that you are an objective observer of your own behavior. A skill that you've had for years and now take for granted should *not* be ignored.

_____   _____

_____   _____

_____   _____

_____   _____

_____   _____

_____   _____

One of my patients named Judy made a similar list. Judy was a twenty-nine-year-old chronic dieter who weighed 178 pounds when I met her. She was a divorced mother of 3- and 5-year-old boys and worked as a secretary at a social welfare agency. At night she was taking classes at a community college with the goal of becoming a commercial artist. In our first session, she tearfully told me of her repeated failures at dieting and described herself using sweeping, negative terms. Thus, she was "a failure," "hopeless," "a fat pig," and so on. Whenever I pointed out any of her obvious strengths, such as her ability to work long hours, her secretarial skills, or artistic abilities, her drive to succeed, or her dedication to her children, she would dismiss it as "no big deal." Carefully I reviewed her strengths with her. Did she know other single mothers who were less devoted to their children than she was? Did she know other working people who did not have the motivation to take night classes? Was everybody else able to draw as well as she did? By pointedly making comparisons, she started to recognize that the attributes that she had taken for granted were worthy of admiration.

Since thinking of herself in terms of her dieting failures was such a deeply ingrained habit, it took some time to develop a more self-nurturing attitude. After Judy became comfortable discussing some of her strengths in our sessions, I had her buy some self-adhesive labels with peel-off backs. On each label she wrote a specific accomplishment or attribute. Her assignment was to put the labels in places where she would see them at various times throughout the day. One went on the underside of the telephone handset at work so she would see it every time she used the telephone. She put another in the compact mirror that she kept in her purse. A third went on the visor of her car and another on the back of the remote control for the VCR. Her instructions were to read what was on the label to herself whenever her eyes fell upon it. Initially Judy objected to this assignment. She felt self-conscious and was afraid that her friends would find the labels and think that she was conceited. Judy started with two labels that she put in inconspicuous places so that she could become more comfortable with the procedure. Gradually she added more labels and actually seemed to be enjoying the process.

Obviously, there is no magic in self-adhesive labels. The idea is to use them so that throughout the day there are tangible reminders of your positive qualities. Take the ten positive attributes you listed above, write each one on a separate label, and put the labels in places where you will see them frequently. If you don't yet have a list of ten positive attributes, give it more thought and complete the list. See if you can use the labels to help remind yourself of your accomplishments Don't worry if it seems artificial or you feel self-conscious. If you push yourself in the beginning, you'll get used to it and eventually learn to appreciate your strengths without the labels.

It also helps to start to say nice things to yourself. Pause, look at something you've just done, and say, "Nice job," to yourself. Don't worry if this seems unnatural. Learning to ride a bicycle, drive a manual transmission car, or any new skill seemed unnatural at first.

Sometimes the lack of self-nurturance may have deeper roots. It may result from a more pervasive poor self-esteem that has its roots in childhood, before the struggles with diet began. If this is the case, counseling or psychotherapy may be helpful as long as the therapist is committed to helping you achieve your goals, even if you have decided that you are not going to diet at this time. It is not helpful to have a therapist who believes that you cannot feel good about yourself unless you are thin.

Start working on self-nurturance now; don't wait until after your therapy is finished. Regardless of whether you are in therapy, don't use low self-esteem as an excuse to avoid working on self-nurturing behaviors and attitudes.

Several of my patients belonged to support groups where they frequently discussed the abuse and deprivation they had suffered as children. Although the attention and concern they received from group members was valuable, sometimes it was too easy to see the support as an indication that they were absolved of the responsibility for making changes in their life. Regardless of their understanding of their childhood suffering, they did not make any progress with their emotional eating until they developed self-nurturing behaviors and attitudes. If you belong to a support group, determine if the group is helping you to recognize, and then move beyond, your painful experiences. If you find that you get attention and support only when you are discussing old hurts and not getting encouragement to try new behaviors, the group may not be helping you.

In the next chapter we will start to identify the specific emotions that are associated with eating. Before we start, you should be clear in your thinking about how you will nurture yourself without food. Don't skip over this assignment.

Identifying Emotions

If you have been faithfully keeping your Emotional Eating Record, you probably have encountered some difficulty filling in the last column—the one where you list the emotion associated with eating. In chapter 2, I asked that you try to identify the emotion, but if you couldn't, to put a question mark in the space and write in the thoughts you had before you decided to eat something. Now your task is to determine the meanings of those question marks.

Identifying emotions can be difficult because you may have been taught to minimize or deny what you were feeling. Boys are frequently told that they shouldn't cry. The message is if you are sad or afraid, you must deny it and certainly not let anyone see. Girls are frequently discouraged from expressing anger. Many women grew up being told to act as if they were happy regardless of how they actually felt. When a child of either sex expresses a negative emotion, an insecure parent may "correct" the child and tell him or her how to feel—for example, "Tell your brother you're sorry" or "Stop making a fuss; that doesn't hurt so bad." Or a parent may mislabel what he or she is feeling about the child, as when an angry parent hits a child and then says, "That hurt me more than it hurt you." If you have had these kinds of experiences, it can become quite difficult to trust your judgment about how you are feeling.

Emotional Confusion

Everybody has had some difficulty identifying the emotion that they are experiencing; occasionally the difficulty indicates a deeper problem called alexithymia, a pervasive inability to experience and express emotions. It has been suggested that for some people with eating disorders, alexithymia is part of a larger confusion about all internal states, including physical states like sensations of hunger and satiety.[1] A twenty-year-old bulimic college woman named Debbie provides a good example of alexithymia and its relationship to eating.

For the past eight years, Debbie's weight typically ranged between 135 and 140 pounds. In seventh grade, after she stopped swimming competitively, her weight spurted to 180 pounds but dropped back to 140 after a few months. Debbie described swimming as "my whole life" because her father was proud of her for it.

Although she was attractively proportioned at her current weight of 136, Debbie felt that she needed to lose 10 pounds. She described herself as having been bulimic since ninth grade. While there were occasional days when she did not binge or purge, she averaged about one binge a day with a maximum of six per day.

As is common with eating-disordered women, Debbie described a distant relationship with her father and a close, almost smothering relationship with her mother. Her father was a retired air force colonel who had become a successful businessman. She described him as analytical and unemotional. For example, after a weekend visit, Debbie told him, "Goodbye, Dad; I love you." He responded, "Thanks." She felt that the last time she got any approval or demonstration of love from him was when she was swimming competitively.

In our early sessions, Debbie would talk about her father in an animated fashion, smiling frequently as though she was describing the plot of a sitcom she had seen on television. When I commented that her feelings must have been hurt by her father's response to her, she cheerfully denied any bad feelings. For the first several months, the only visible sign of emotion during our sessions were tears when she described how her bulimia hurt and disappointed her mother. She denied that *she* had any bad feelings about her bulimia or any of the problems in her life; the tears were only about her mother's disappointment.

As our sessions progressed, a pattern of emotional responding emerged, and Debbie's crying became more frequent. When I asked her why she was crying or offered a possible interpretation of the tears, she would look helpless and could only say that she was "mazzled"— her term to describe her profound inner emotional confusion. She seemed puzzled, and occasionally annoyed, that I spent so much of our time talking about her emotions, defining various emotional terms, and trying to help her identify what she was feeling. I was pleased when she started one session by announcing that she had felt sad after the previous session when we had been discussing her father. During the ensuing weeks, she started to identify other emotions: she was bored with school, frequently felt anger toward her father for being so distant, and was fearful any time she felt that her mother might be withdrawing from her. The course of treatment was fitful, characterized by almost as many relapses as improvements, but Debbie's gradual progress in identifying and experiencing her emotions was accompanied by increasing control over her bulimia. Fortunately, alexithymia is rare. It's likely that you will have a much easier time identifying your emotions than Debbie did.

The Psychology of Emotions

To start, it will help to see how emotions are conceptualized and then become familiar with the terms psychologists use to define the different emotions. After forty-three years of studying emotions, Richard Lazarus concluded:

> When we react with an emotion, especially a strong one, every fiber of our being is likely to be engaged—our attention and thought, our needs and desire, and even our bodies. The reaction tells us that an important value or goal has been engaged and is being harmed, placed at risk, or advanced. From an emotional reaction we can learn much about what a person has at stake in the encounter with the environment or in life in general, how that person interprets self and world, and how harms, threats, and challenges are coped with. . . .
> . . . If we pay attention, emotions can inform us about psychological processes that might otherwise not have been noticed or their significance grasped.[2]

Although there is some controversy about the relationship between the physical and mental components of emotion, most psychologists agree that emotions have both aspects. We implicitly recognize the physical component when we use phases like "it took my breath away." Some of the bodily changes that can be associated with emotion include:

1. channeling of the blood supply to the muscles and brain
2. slowing down of stomach and intestinal activity
3. increase in heart rate and blood pressure
4. widening of the pupils of the eyes
5. increase in rates of metabolism and respiration
6. decrease in electrical resistance of the skin
7. increase in the speed of the blood's ability to clot
8. "goose pimples" resulting from the erection of hairs on the skin.[3]

According to Dr. Lazarus, physiological arousal is most obvious in anger and fear, but other emotions are characterized by more subtle physiological changes.

One widely held theory, based on the work of social psychologist Stanley Schachter, suggests that all emotions are characterized by a diffuse state of physiological arousal that includes many of the symptoms just listed.[4] According to Dr. Schachter, the difference between one emotion and another results from the source of the arousal and one's response to it. For example, if you think your car is about to crash, the arousal would be experienced as fear. If the arousal follows a verbal insult from your brother or sister, the resulting emotion would be labeled anger. Emotions are rarely this uncomplicated, however. If you are insulted by a large, menacing stranger, you may feel both fearful and angry.

Although emotions can be intense physical experiences, frequently they are difficult to understand. Sometimes you may feel the physical arousal of an emotion but not be able to identify the source. This type of "free-floating" emotional state is distressing since it doesn't have any obvious explanation. When you were using the Emotional Eating Record, you may have jotted down several emotions occurring together or in a brief period of time. Another possible source of difficulty in labeling emotions is that they tend to fluctuate. Anxiety that you experience when you think your car will crash quickly changes to a sense of relief when you realize that you weren't hurt. Or feelings of anger directed to a child may be quickly replaced by guilt when you think about the harsh words you just said to the child. When identifying our emotional states and relating them to eating, it is important to realize that we are dealing with combinations of continuously changing, complex mental and physical states. To make sense out of your emotional eating, consider the emotions separately even though, at any one time, you may experience several.

The Language of Emotions

Part of the difficulty of identifying emotions results from the large number of words in the English language that describe identical or very similar emotional states. *Stress, fear, anxiety, worry, tension, nervousness, panic, terror,* and *apprehension* identify similar or overlapping emotions. Our usage of these words is somewhat idiosyncratic. Two people riding in the same car, having the same close call as the driver swerves and just misses an oncoming truck, might use different terms to describe their emotional state following the near accident. For the purposes of casual conversation, it probably doesn't matter if you were to describe your reaction as fear, terror, or panic; any of the terms will do. But for your purposes, you will need to be more consistent in defining emotions so that you can discover your typical patterns and track your progress.

Since there are dozens, perhaps hundreds of terms used to describe emotions, it will be simpler to focus on the emotions that are most commonly linked with eating. In his 1989 review of thirty years of clinical and experimental studies, Richard Ganley found the following terms linked to eating: *anxiety, depression, loneliness, boredom, stress in family and occupational relationships, helplessness and hopelessness, separation from an important person, frustration, feeling isolated, nervousness, feeling blue, repressed sexuality, impulsivity, tiredness, feeling sorry for oneself, worthlessness,* and *unhappiness.* Obviously many of these terms refer to the same emotional states. He summarized the findings: "A major determinant of emotional eating is its ability to reduce negative emotions such as anger, depression, loneliness, boredom, and anxiety."[5]

Consistent with Dr. Ganley's review, I have used the terms *depression, anxiety, boredom, loneliness,* and *anger* to identify the negative emotions that have been linked to eating. It is possible that some of your eating may be linked to another, less common emotion like guilt or jealousy. Also, virtually all of the research reviewed by Dr. Ganley focused on negative emotions. He suggested that future research should investigate possible relationships between positive emotions and eating. (In chapter 11 we will look at love and eating.)

Identifying Emotions

Dr. Lazarus suggests that most emotions start with an interpersonal transaction—for example, an argument between coworkers, a tender moment between lovers, or a mother telling her son to clean up his room. Think about your own interpersonal transactions. Very brief or businesslike transactions (getting a telephone number from the information operator, for example) are likely to be free of emotions. Most of the rest will elicit some emotion. When you are trying to identify an emotion, looking at recent interactions with others is a good place to start.

Typically when you have an interpersonal situation in which you are thwarted, the result will be a negative emotion. According to Dr. Lazarus, the negative emotions differ from each other because each is a "separate and distinct reaction to diverse forms of thwarting." Each reflects a different relationship between the person and the environment and a different pattern of how the situation is evaluated by the person. In order to identify your emotions, look at the interpersonal theme, your subjective evaluation of it, the behavior (what you do), and your body's reaction associated with each emotion. But before you do this, get a week's worth (or more) of the Emotional Eating Record. After reading the definition and characteristics of each emotion, you can refer to the records to reevaluate the frequency of your eating associated with each. Keep in mind that there is nothing unusual or pathological about any of these emotions. They are common, virtually universal experiences.

Sadness and Depression

Sadness and depression are similar but not identical concepts. Although most of the research in this area uses the term *depression,* it will be helpful to distinguish between them so that we can understand the relationship of either to eating. According to Dr. Lazarus, the core theme of sadness is "having experienced an irrevocable loss."[6] Most theorizing about depression, going back to Freud, has also revolved around the theme of loss.[7] Psychiatrist Aaron Beck suggested that seven different kinds of losses can lead to sadness:

1. Loss of a tangible object or person that is valued (e.g., your spouse leaves you)
2. An intangible loss such as lowered self-esteem produced by an insult
3. A reversal in value (e.g., the puppy you bought brings you more problems than pleasure)
4. A discrepancy between what you expected and what you received (e.g., a disappointment like getting socks for Christmas)
5. Expectation of a future loss (e.g., thinking about the death of your mother while she is still alive)
6. A hypothetical or possible loss (e.g., thinking about the possibility that the stock you bought will decrease in value)
7. An inaccurately perceived loss (e.g., you think you have been criticized by your boss when he made a neutral comment)[8]

When you are sad, you tend to withdraw into yourself. The typical body posture of the sad person—eyes cast downward, slumped shoulders, forward-leaning body—seems to express the withdrawal from the world and shrinking of one's identity.

Depression is more complex than sadness. Although it, like sadness, focuses on loss, it includes broader implications of the loss for one's whole life. If you lose a job, you may feel the loss and are sad. But if you also feel worthless, ashamed, anxious about your future, and hopeless about ever finding another job, you are depressed. Sometimes following a loss, you may not consciously describe yourself as sad yet still be depressed. You might describe yourself as tired or in pain, or others might describe you as cranky or irritable. Although it may not be obvious, often there is a loss behind this type of depressed behavior.

Charles was a fifty-three-year-old retired policeman who denied being sad yet clearly seemed depressed. Six years ago, he had injured his back while climbing a fence and took a disability retirement. Not only did he lose his job; he lost many of the intangible aspects of a career. In the past, he thought of himself as a cop; most of his friends were police, many of his off-duty activities were related to being a police officer, and his role in the family was as the strong, competent breadwinner. All of this was lost when Charles retired, yet his notion of how he should behave did not allow for any expression of sadness. He equated sadness with self-pity and weakness. Despite his denial, his stooped posture, sense of hopelessness about the future, "tiredness," and continuing reports of vague pains were indications of depression related to his losses.

In the best-seller *Feeling Good: The New Mood Therapy,* David Burns describes sadness as a desirable, normal emotion resulting from a realistic image of a negative event involving loss or disappointment.[9] Although it isn't pleasant, this feeling is desirable and "adds depth to the meaning of life." Depression, on the other hand, results from distortions in thinking about the negative event; after a loss, you think, "This is a calamity. I'll never be happy again."

Can you recognize times when you were sad or depressed? Try to identify the loss and the thinking that set off the emotion. Was it sadness, with a realistic appraisal of the loss, or depression, with exaggerated, sweeping negative predictions about your miserable future? Go back to your Emotional Eating Record for the past week and review the Emotions column. Do you have many entries that indicate sadness, depression, or similar terms? How about fatigue or being tired? Try to recall the circumstances to determine if sadness or depression describes what you were feeling, and write in the appropriate term. Then for every question mark or blank space, check the thoughts that you were having. Did the thoughts revolve around a real or imagined loss (review Dr. Beck's list to help identify losses)? If so, the emotion was probably sadness. In addition to the loss, were there thoughts about how bad or worthless you are, or hopelessness about the future, helplessness (you are powerless to improve your situation), tiredness, and feeling sorry for yourself? If you felt sadness, plus any or all of these related thoughts and feelings, *depression* would be a better description. If either fits, write it in the Emotions column.

Fear and Anxiety

Fear and anxiety have played a central role in most psychological theories from Freud to the existentialists to the behaviorists. Although there are major disagreements about the causes, the experience seems to be almost universal. Psychoanalyst Wilhelm Stekel listed the intense anxieties suffered by major historical figures: Augustus Caesar was afraid of thunder, Erasmus of fish, Frederick the Great had an aversion for new clothing, Mozart was afraid of the sound of a trumpet, Schopenhauer was afraid of the sight of a razor, and Edgar

Allen Poe, Schumann, and Chopin were afraid of the dark.[10]
The distinction between fear and anxiety that most theorists
make is similar to the difference between sadness and depression. Fear, like sadness, is thought of as a purer emotional
experience. It may be a basic alarm to a very real, present
danger. Fear is found in all cultures and races, as well as in
other species. Charles Darwin suggested that fear was necessary for the survival of the species.[11] In contrast, definitions of
anxiety are more variable and are more likely to reflect theo-
retical influences. A Freudian definition of anxiety would focus on the unconscious forces that are threatening to emerge
into consciousness; a behavioral definition might stress the
specific types of physiological arousal or the degree to which a
person avoids the anxiety-provoking stimulus. Its not just the
theorists who disagree about anxiety. Your experience of anxiety is likely to be somewhat different from mine. Despite these
differences, there is a common theme to everyone's anxiety: a
sense of apprehension or worry about a future event that will
be unpleasant or dangerous. Something bad is going to happen to you; you may or may not know what is going to happen
or when, but, regardless, there is a sense of impending disaster. Since it seems that you have no control over this unpre-
dictable, unpleasant future event, you become preoccupied
with it, and anything that you are trying to do now is disrupted. The physiological arousal you experience when anxious is your body preparing itself to deal with the imminent
disaster that you think is about to befall you.

Again, go back to your Emotional Eating Record and look
through your entries in the Emotions column. First, search out
all the fear and anxiety synonyms (stress, panic, phobic, tension, worry, and others). See if you can more accurately label
them as fear (specific, immediate, physical danger) or anxiety
(generalized, uncertain threat to your well-being). Also review
the question marks and empty spaces in the Emotions column.

Try to recall the situation at the time, and see if fear or anxiety describes what you were feeling before eating. Write in *fear* or *anxiety* if either is appropriate.

Boredom and Loneliness

Neither boredom nor loneliness is a "pure" emotion. Although either could be broken down into more basic emotional components, they will be useful in helping us to discover patterns of emotional eating. Boredom and loneliness are not internal feeling states. Both are defined largely in terms of perceived deficits in the environment. With boredom, there is a lack of interesting activities; with loneliness, there is a lack of satisfying interpersonal relationships. According to Richard Stuart, the former psychological director for Weight Watchers:

> The typical bored eater is the housewife/mother who has limited variety in her daily routine. She spends most of her time engaged in tasks that are crucial, but lacking in excitement or intellectual challenge. . . . Eating is an end-in-itself that rescues her from the tedium of the hour.[12]

Although there has been much psychological research done on boredom, several theorists have suggested that being bored requires more than just a lack of interesting activities. Behavioral psychologist B. F. Skinner stated that boredom occurred when there was nothing to do because the situation didn't allow it or an external force prevented the individual from doing something.[13] The founder of Gestalt therapy, Frederick ("Fritz") Perls, said essentially the same thing: boredom occurs when you have to focus attention on something that lacks interest (like doing housework) while being blocked from attending to something that would be more interesting (like reading a book).[14] Doing nothing is not necessarily boring;

sometimes it's actually fun. It is only the sense that you are being prevented from doing something else that would be interesting that produces the bored feelings. Thus, the housewife/mother that Dr. Stuart describes is prevented from doing more interesting activities by the responsibilities and expectations that are implicit in her role. Subjectively, boredom feels as if time goes by in slow motion. You check the clock frequently and are disappointed that it has only been a few minutes since the last time you looked. When you are bored, you will yawn frequently and may feel tired. You may eat to relieve the boredom, but ultimately eating provides only temporary and unsatisfying relief.

Loneliness has been defined as "the absence, or perceived absence, of satisfying social relationships, accompanied by symptoms of psychological distress."[15] Jeffrey Young, a psychologist who has been studying loneliness, describes lonely individuals as being without:

A "caring" person to depend on
Someone who understands them
The opportunity to express their private feelings to another person
A close group of friends they feel part of
Someone who needs them and wants their love
Other people who share their values and interests
Friends to share enjoyable activities
Friendships they had at another point in their lives and have been unable to replace
A particular person they lost
Collegial relationships at work
A sense of trust with close friends
Physical intimacy on a regular basis

His definition would not include hermits and many "loners," individuals who enjoy solitude, since these people are not experiencing psychological distress. They seem to be content despite the absence of interpersonal relationships. In contrast, people who deny being lonely but report that they are not experiencing the satisfactions of interpersonal relationships and show signs of psychological distress would fit the definition despite their denial. This psychological distress of loneliness can take many forms. Alcohol and drug abuse, depression, anxiety, and sleeplessness, combined with an absence of satisfying social relations, would justify the term *lonely*. Thus, the actual subjective experience may not be different from one of the other emotions. Loneliness is a unique experience because of the absence of satisfying relationships.

To identify boredom and loneliness, review column 4 on your Emotional Eating Record, but this time also look at column 2. For each blank space or question mark in column 4, check column 2 to see where you were and if you were alone or with other people. Some environments are more likely to elicit feelings of boredom than others. The Location column may provide clues to help you identify eating associated with boredom. Perhaps sitting in a lecture hall listening to an uninspiring instructor is boring, and you brought a snack for stimulation. Or maybe some of your emotional eating routinely takes place in the car as you do your daily commute to work. Also check to see if you were alone or with other people. If you were alone, review Dr. Young's twelve deficits to see if they describe your circumstances at the time. If you wrote your thoughts in column 4, did they revolve around any of these interpersonal themes? Write in *bored* or *lonely* where appropriate.

Anger

According to Aristotle, "Anger may be defined as a belief that we, or our friends, have been unfairly slighted, which causes in us both painful feelings and a desire or impulse for revenge."[16] This definition, more than two thousand years old, well summarizes much of the current psychological theorizing about anger. Anger differs from the other negative emotions because someone else is blamed for the harm or threat that you are experiencing. You believe that the person could have acted differently so that you would not be suffering now. Even when he or she is not present, when you think about the person you may find yourself getting angry again and planning revenge. When you are angry, your physical arousal is usually apparent to others. You may look red and flushed; your eyelids may become narrowed and jaws clenched; your whole body stiffens. When you are talking with or about the person who is the object of your anger, your voice changes; you may become louder and more forceful, or perhaps your speech becomes slow and calculating but no less intense.

Sometimes when you feel angry, you inhibit the expression of anger because the object of your anger is too powerful and might retaliate. When the direct expression of anger is not safe, the angry person may express it indirectly using passive-aggressive tactics. For example, it might not be safe to express your anger directly by telling a dictatorial boss exactly what you think of him, but you can "forget" to complete an assignment, do a poor job, or turn it in late.

Anger is an emotion that is experienced frequently and strongly. One survey found that more than three-fourths of those polled had been angry within the past week, and they rated the intensity of their anger as 6.7 on a 10-point scale.[17] Can you think of recent situations that have made you angry? What do you do when you are angry? Do you explode, yell, hit things? Do you become quiet, brooding, and sullen with a chip on your shoulder? Or do you prefer not to be angry, choosing to overlook the slight you have experienced? If you do not believe that anger is acceptable (a common condition among women socialized into the traditional female role), it may be hard to recognize angry feelings. Go back to your Emotional Eating Record for the past week and check the Emotions column. Look for terms like *annoyed* or *irritated,* and change them to *anger.* Each time there was a question mark or a blank space, see if you can recall what was happening prior to eating. See if you wrote any thoughts in the Emotions column. Were the thoughts about "unfairness" or being slighted? If there aren't any thoughts in the Emotions column, try to reconstruct in your mind the events that were taking place to see if you were feeling slighted or treated unfairly. If this type of theme characterizes your thoughts at the time or your recollection of the events that were taking place, it is likely that the emotion you were experiencing was anger. If so, write it in.

What Kind of Emotional Eater Are You?

Assuming that you have kept track of your emotional eating for at least seven days (not necessarily in a row), you should now be able to determine which emotions are the most significant triggers for eating. Even without doing a careful count, you may already have a pretty good idea of which emotions are your triggers. Nevertheless, go through your records and make tally marks in the appropriate space, count the marks, and write the totals here:

_____   Sadness/depression
_____   Fear/anxiety
_____   Boredom
_____   Loneliness
_____   Anger

If no pattern has emerged, reread the definitions and descriptions of the different emotions and keep your Emotional

Eating Record for another week. Before you move on, glance through the records one more time. Look at the Location/ People column to see if there are any particular places or people associated with your emotional eating. This will be useful information later.

If you are clear about which emotion or combination of emotions is responsible for most of your emotional eating, then you may turn directly to the chapter that deals with it. You can come back and read the intervening chapters after you started working on the most significant emotion. If you are not sure of the emotion, read the following chapters in sequence. There will be more information to help you identify each emotion.

7

Depression and Eating

Depression is sometimes referred to as the common cold of mental illness, but it is probably more accurate to think of it as a range of disorders, starting with the less severe, short-lived variety analogous to the common cold but also including more serious disorders. A depressed mood may slow you down, but it does not prevent routine functioning. Clinical depression, on the other hand, can result in significant impairment, possibly resulting in suicide. Clinical depression is quite common, especially among women. According to one estimate, one in four American women will have a major depressive episode in her lifetime—two times the rate for men.[1]

Most depressions, regardless of whether they are the common variety or a more disabling psychiatric disorder, affect eating. The third edition, revised, of the psychiatric diagnostic manual, *Diagnostic and Statistical Manual of Mental Disorders,* (DSM-III-R), includes changes in appetite or weight for virtually all of the depressive disorders.[2] For example, "significant weight loss or weight gain when not dieting" is a criterion for major depressive episode and "poor appetite or overeating" is a criterion for dysthymia, a less serious type of depression. This manual also describes depressed mood as an associated feature of bulimia nervosa, the binge-purge eating disorder. Several research studies have demonstrated a link between eating disorders and depression. One study of female bulimics found that 70 percent had an episode of major depression at some time during their lives.[3] Other studies have documented depressed mood in anorexics.[4] The link between depression and eating may be at least partially biological. Researchers Richard and Judith Wurtman suggest that the neurotransmitter serotonin may be involved in both depression and eating binges. Several antidepressants, including Prozac, work by facilitating serotonin neurotransmission. Carbohydrate-rich foods that are often used for snacks or binges also increase the production of serotonin. The Wurtmans note that not all obesity may be related to carbohydrates, but for some people, carbohydrate snacking may serve as a type of antidepressant.[5]

Whether your emotional eating is linked to a clinical depression or just ordinary depression, the good news is that all types of depression can be effectively treated. (I will assume that your depression does not warrant any of the DSM-III-R diagnoses, but if you are being treated for clinical depression, you can still use the methods in this chapter. The only caution I suggest is that you show this chapter to the clinician who is treating you.)

Recall the distinction between sadness and depression. Both revolve around the theme of loss, but sadness is a healthy response to loss. Sadness has limits. After a period of sadness, the loss is accepted, and you resume normal living. Depression is different in several ways. In addition to sadness, there are many other symptoms: a loss of self-esteem, an overall sense of pessimism about the future, decreased energy, sleep difficulties, and perhaps physical pain. Emotional eating is more likely to be associated with depression than with sadness. Check your Emotional Eating Record. If you find that some of your emotional eating results from sadness and not depression, you'll be pleased to know that sadness is temporary; you will feel better before too long. In the interim, to help cope with the sadness, skip the next section of this chapter, which deals with depressed thinking, and go on to the Changing Behavior section, which contains suggestions for behavior change that are helpful for both sadness and depression.

If your emotional eating is associated with depression, you first need to identify your patterns of thinking that produce depression so that you can change them before you can change your behavior.

Depressed Thinking

Some of the most promising work in treating depression has developed from the work of psychiatrist Aaron Beck. Dr. Beck's approach, called cognitive therapy, identifies three common themes in the thoughts of depressed patients: a negative view of the world, a negative self-concept, and a negative or pessimistic view of the future.[6] You may be thinking, "Of course I'll have negative thoughts if I've lost my job [or spouse, or bank account, or any other significant loss]." According to cognitive therapy, your feelings are not caused by the event itself; rather, you feel bad because of your thoughts about the event. This is not a new idea. Almost two thousand years ago, Epictetus, the Greek physician, said, "Men are not moved by things but the views they take of them." For a more contemporary example, watch the news on television after a major flood, fire, or other disaster. Among the people who have lost their homes, some will see themselves and their future as hopeless; others will be sad about their loss but ready to go to work to rebuild their lives. The loss is the same, but the thinking about the loss is different, and the emotion follows the thinking.

Cognitive therapy is not just a repackaged version of positive thinking. I am not going to tell you to "put on a happy face," or "smile and the whole world smiles with you." When you are depressed, this type of encouragement seems phony and is rarely helpful. Instead, cognitive therapy focuses on patterns of illogical thinking that lead to the negative thoughts that cause the depressed mood. The goal of cognitive therapy is to identify and correct the illogical thinking. Think about the last time you were depressed. The content of your thinking probably revolved around a loss that you experienced (you might want to review Dr. Beck's list of the types of losses in chapter 6). Experiencing a loss is ample justification for feeling sad. Being depressed, however, requires illogical thinking about the loss. Dr. Beck describes the sequence of cognitive events leading to depression as follows:

After experiencing loss (either as the result of an actual, obvious event or insidious deprivations) the depression-prone person begins to appraise his experiences in a negative way. He over interprets his experiences in terms of defeat or deprivation. He regards himself as deficient, inadequate, unworthy, and is prone to attribute unpleasant occurrences to a deficiency in himself. As he looks ahead, he anticipates that his present difficulties or suffering will continue indefinitely. He foresees a life of unremitting hardship, frustration, and deprivation. Since he attributes his difficulties to his own defects, he blames himself and becomes increasingly self-critical. The patient's experiences in living thus activate cognitive patterns revolving around the theme of loss. The various emotional, motivational, behavioral, and vegetative (sleep, appetite disturbances) phenomena of depression flow from these negative self-evaluations.[7]

In order to use Dr. Beck's techniques, I'm going to ask you to do something that may take some practice: learn to think about your thinking. Most of the time when we think, we thing about something. Right now, you're probably thinking about what you've just read in this book, or perhaps your mind wandered and you started to think about what you need to do when you stop reading. This is the *content* of your thought. In cognitive therapy, you will focus on *patterns* of thought, independent of the topic you are thinking about. Each of us has automatic thoughts, typical patterns or well-worn channels of thought, regardless of the content of the thoughts. For many people, the hardest part of cognitive therapy is learning to recognize their automatic thoughts. Once you are able to identify these thoughts, you will examine them logically and learn to substitute more realistic judgments. Since thinking about thinking has the potential to get you going around in circles, leaving you thoroughly confused, I'm going to provide plenty of spaces for you to write your thoughts down. When they are on paper, they become more tangible and easier to examine.

Recall the last time you were depressed. It may help to look at your Emotional Eating Record to remember the circumstances. See if you can identify the negative thoughts that *preceded* the idea to get something to eat. This is important because it is easy to focus on the thoughts about food and eating. Instead, try to visualize where you were and what you were doing before you had the urge to get something to eat. See if you can identify your negative view of the world (e.g., "Life stinks"), your negative view of yourself (e.g., "I'm a hopeless loser"), or your negative view of the future (e.g., "It's never going to get better"). When I gave a forty-four-year-old patient named Margaret this assignment, she found that her thoughts before eating fit the pattern exactly.

Margaret was a nurse who had a history of depressive moods. Almost any interpersonal rebuff, regardless of how trivial, would provoke a depressed mood lasting from several hours to a week or more. If a patient complained that Margaret was slow in answering the buzzer or that a blood draw was painful, Margaret would start thinking a series of negative thoughts about herself and, eventually, about the future. One day a patient asked her, in an annoyed tone, "What took you so long?" Margaret stammered an answer about being busy with another patient and then began several hours of an internal monologue in which she criticized her ability to work efficiently and then remembered the difficulty she had with an advanced course in nursing school. Next, she recalled that her husband had criticized her that morning for not filling up the car with gas. As she continued to find further evidence of her inadequacies, Margaret projected into the future, concluding that she was hopeless, her life would always be one disaster after another, and the world would be a better place if she were dead. Within five minutes after the criticism from the patient, Margaret was eating. She snacked on a bag of cookies she had in her locker and bought a few bags of M&Ms from the candy machine during her break that afternoon. When she got home, she had dinner, which was followed by an evening of television viewing and sneaky snacking. Once she started emotional eating, Margaret had further "proof" of her inadequacies. Not only was she a stupid, incompetent nurse and thoughtless wife; she was also a hopeless, fat slob. These automatic thoughts, triggered by the patient's criticism, produced Margaret's depressed mood and emotional eating.

Perhaps you're thinking that Margaret is exaggerating or blowing things out of proportion. If so, give yourself a pat on the back. You have recognized that she is making several logical errors in drawing conclusions about her competence as a nurse, wife, and human being on the basis of a single critical comment from an annoyed patient. Now the trick will be to learn to identify your own automatic thoughts, recognize the distortions in these thoughts, and then to develop methods to combat them.

Identifying Automatic Thoughts

Automatic thoughts are triggered by an antecedent (an event preceding another)—usually a stimulus from the environment. Frequently they are obvious, like the patient who asked Margaret, "What took you so long?" Criticisms and insults are often antecedents. Sometimes the antecedent is more subtle: you greet a co-worker as you walk by, and she doesn't respond. Occasionally there is no apparent stimulus from the environment. You can be by yourself, humming a song, which may be an antecedent. Whatever the source, the antecedent elicits an automatic thought. For Margaret, there were several thoughts of inadequacy and worthlessness. In a situation where a co-worker doesn't respond to your greeting, the thought is likely to be, "She doesn't like me." If you are humming a song that is associated with an old boyfriend, the thought might be, "I'll never find anyone who will love me as much as he did." The third part of the sequence is the emotion. In these examples, the emotion is depression. Now, using this antecedent-thought-emotion (A-T-E) sequence, go back to your last instance of emotional eating triggered by depression, and see if you can determine the antecedent, thought, and emotion. Write them in below:

Antecedent: _____

Thought(s): _____

Emotion: ___*Depression*___

Identifying the A-T-E sequence will take some practice. In the next few days, use your eating as a cue. When you find yourself bingeing, sneaky snacking, or grazing, see if you can determine the antecedent, thought, and emotion. Record the next two instances in the spaces below. Don't be surprised if antecedents elicit thoughts that result in emotions other than depression. We will work on A-T-E sequences associated with other emotions in later chapters.

Date ____Time _____   Date ____Time _____

Antecedent: _____   Antecedent: _____

Thought: _____   Thought: _____

Emotion: _____   Emotion: _____

Changing Thinking

Once you have identified the thought that follows the antecedent, you may find yourself feeling a little foolish because when you say it out loud or write it on paper, it seems illogical. Our task now is to identify patterns of irrational thinking. Several cognitive theorists have developed lists of common distortions. The one that I find most useful is Dr. Burns's Ten Forms of Twisted Thinking, described below with minor modifications.[8] As you read through the list, see if you can identify distortions in the thoughts of your three A-T-E sequences you've completed.

Ten Forms of Twisted Thinking

1. *All-or-nothing thinking.* This is black-or-white, no-shades-of-gray thinking. Dieters are notorious for this type of thinking. Either you are on your diet totally or completely off it. One cookie and you think, "That's it. I've blown my diet."

2. *Overgeneralization.* On the basis of a single instance or one negative example, you make a sweeping generalization. Frequently you can detect the presence of

an overgeneralization by the appearance of the words *always* or *never*. Thus, after failing to lose weight on a new diet, you think, "I *always* screw up."

3. *Mental filter.* In a situation that has many different facets, you focus on the negative detail, to the exclusion of everything else. For example, in a class you are taking, you get an A on a term paper. Although the professor wrote many positive comments, you think only about the grammatical error that he corrected.

4. *Discounting the positive.* When something good happens, you ignore or minimize it. Common examples include statements like, "It's no big deal; anyone could have done that", or, "It was okay, but what I should have done was . . ."

5. *Jumping to conclusions.* You reach a conclusion, invariably a negative one, although there is little or no evidence to support it. You assume that a friend is angry with you when she doesn't return your call ("mind reading") or you predict that since you are depressed today, the rest of your life will be absolutely miserable ("fortune telling").

6. *Magnification.* Negative events or characteristics are blow out of proportion. You are on a diet; your friends ordered a pizza, and you eat a slice and spend the rest of the day brooding about having "blown" your diet.

7. *Emotional reasoning.* You experience a negative emotion like anger and assume that someone has done something nasty to you. You misinterpret the reality of the situation because of your emotional state.

8. "Should" *statements.* If you use the word *should* (or *must* or *ought*) directed toward yourself—"I *should* eat cottage cheese for lunch" it is likely that you will

set up arbitrary standards, which will result in disappointment and guilt when they are not met. If the *should* is directed to another person—"He *should* know how I feel"—you are likely to be disappointed and angry. It is perfectly reasonable to have preferences, but *shoulds* are usually unreasonable absolutes.

9. *Labeling.* Everyone makes mistakes. You may do something foolish, but that does not make you a fool. After doing something foolish, you will undoubtedly go on to do dozens of perfectly sensible things. Attaching a label to yourself (or someone else) on the basis of a single behavior, or even several behaviors, is unreasonable.

10. *Personalization and blame.* Personalization occurs when you accept responsibility for something that you have had no control over. If you have large hips, you blame yourself, but it is likely that your genetic makeup is largely responsible. Blame is equally unrealistic, but here the responsibility is attributed to someone else. For example, the reason that you can't lose weight is that your overweight husband refuses to go on a diet.

As you read though the list, you probably could identify a few of your habitual thoughts but might be a little confused because more than one type of twisted thinking applies. Don't worry; frequently there is overlap. For example, labeling ("I don't have any willpower") may imply all-or-nothing thinking (after all, you probably have exercised *some* willpower in the past) and a *should* statement ("I should have been able to resist eating that doughnut"). It is not necessary for you to identify precisely each type of twisted thinking. What is important is that you start to dispute, and ultimately correct, the irrational thinking that produces the depression and emotional eating.

I asked Margaret to write down her thoughts after the incident with the impatient patient. This is what she wrote:

Date _Thursday_ Time _3:30 pm_ Antecedent _Patient complained that I was slow_

Thought(s): _1. I'm always slow_

2. I'm inefficient, I'll never be a good nurse

3. I got a D in microbiology when I was in nursing school

4. I'm a lousy wife, I should have put gas in the car

Using the list of twisted thoughts, I asked Margaret to identify her illogical thinking and to write in more reasonable alternatives:

1. This is an overgeneralization. I am sometimes slow but often I am as fast as anyone else.

2. This is labeling and jumping to conclusions. Even if I was inefficient this time, it doesn't mean that I am an inefficient person. It is illogical for me to try to predict the future. I have been a successful *nurse for seven years. There is no evidence to suggest that I won't be a good nurse in the future.*

3. This is a mental filter. I did get a 'D' in microbiology but I had a B+ average in all my nursing classes.

4. This is labeling again, and a should statement. Even if I forget to do something, it is illogical to conclude that I'm a lousy wife. It would be nice if I could remember to do all my chores, but there is no sacred edict that says I "SHOULD" always do this.

Now it's your turn. In the first column below, write in the thoughts from the three A-T-E examples above. In the second column, identify the type(s) of twisted thinking that goes into that thought, and in the third column, write in a more rational response

Date _____ Time _____ Antecedent _____

Thought	Type of Twisted Thinking	Rational Response

Date _____ Time _____ Antecedent _____

Thought	Type of Twisted Thinking	Rational Response
_____	_____	_____
_____	_____	_____
_____	_____	_____
_____	_____	_____

Date _____ Time _____ Antecedent _____

Thought	Type of Twisted Thinking	Rational Response
_____	_____	_____
_____	_____	_____
_____	_____	_____
_____	_____	_____

Perhaps you're a little skeptical. You're not sure it's worth the effort to do all this writing—or you may have a hard time identifying depressive thinking that occurs before emotional eating. Margaret had the same objections. Initially she argued that she didn't have enough time to stop what she was doing and make notes. When I gave her 3 × 5 cards and told her that she didn't need to write complete sentences, only phrases that summarized the thought, she objected that it was hard to identify the thought that preceded the urge to eat. We spent some time reconstructing the circumstances that were taking place when she ate. When she was able to describe them, she was able to pinpoint the responsible thought. Then we could discuss the irrationality of that thought and replace it with a more rational thought using the procedure I have described. With practice, she was able to do this without my assistance. After several weeks, she would start our sessions by telling me about an automatic thought that she had during the previous week and how she rebutted it to herself. The frequency of her depressed moods and emotional eating decreased as she did this.

Try to do these exercises. It's *not* sufficient just to read about twisted thinking. In order to change well-established thinking patterns, you have to identify them and write them down so that you can examine them objectively and then dispute them. If you need a more detailed description of the procedure or a fuller critique of the illogical nature of the ten types of twisted thinking, it might be helpful to consult one of Dr. Burns's books.[9]

Changing Behavior

Research on the effectiveness of cognitive therapy demonstrates that changing automatic thoughts will greatly reduce depression.[10] To speed your progress, there is a second approach, entirely consistent with cognitive therapy, that you can use while you are working on changing your thinking. Exercise also has been supported by many research studies.

Most dieters have been told repeatedly that they need to exercise to lose weight, but most of these exhortations fall on deaf ears. Exercise is seen as a physically painful experience that must be repeated endlessly for the rest of one's life. In addition to the physical discomfort, exercise may conjure up negative images of failure at competitive sports, embarrassment in gym classes, feeling clumsy or uncoordinated, having to wear overly revealing outfits, sweating profusely, or other unhappy past experiences. If the dieter was able to overcome these barriers and begin an exercise program, frequently he or she would get discouraged with the slow rate of weight loss that followed.

Regardless of whether you want to lose weight or are perfectly content at your current weight, exercise improves self-concept and decreases depression. In one study, forty clinically depressed women were assigned to either a running group, a weight-lifting group, or a waiting-list group that did not participate in exercise. The runners and weight-lifters attended three or four sessions a week for eight weeks. During the exercise period, the runners ran or walked around an indoor track for twenty minutes, and the weight lifters spent twenty minutes using a Universal Exercise Machine. For both groups, the sessions lasted between thirty and forty minutes including warmups. The results of exercising were clearly significant. Before treatment, the three groups were equally depressed. As treatment progressed, the two exercise groups became less depressed, and the improved mood was maintained throughout the one-year follow-up. There were no differences between running and weight lifting: both types of exercise decreased depression.[11] The same exercise treatments were also shown to improve self-concept in clinically depressed women.[12] In both studies, improvements were found, even though the exercising was not intense enough to improve cardiovascular fitness. In other words, you don't have to be an athlete or push yourself to your limit in order to get the benefits.

The findings of these studies and several dozen others demonstrate that regular exercise, even if it is not strenuous, improves mood and self-concept. If exercise is so beneficial, why aren't all depressed people exercising? The paradox is that when people are depressed, they have less energy. Even routine tasks like household chores become more effortful when you are depressed. If it is hard to muster up the energy to make the bed, the idea of exercising can seem overwhelming. Using the cognitive perspective described above, it will become apparent that much of this hesitancy is a result of twisted thinking. Let's look at some of your assumptions about exercise.

If you found yourself agreeing with the negative images from previous experiences, it's important to recognize that an exercise program you create for yourself will be quite different from your earlier experiences. Since it will not be part of a gym class or a sport, there will be no competition; you do not have to compare your performance with anyone else's. If you prefer, you can exercise on your own so that you don't have to worry about embarrassment or the outfit you will wear. If you think of yourself as clumsy or unathletic, that should not present any problems since a good exercise program does not require that you play a sport or do anything requiring a skill. When it is your own exercise program, the only difficulties are likely to be finding an activity that you can do comfortably, finding the time to do it, and becoming motivated enough to follow through consistently.

The research suggests that increasing muscle mass or improving cardiovascular fitness is not necessary for improvements in mood and self-concept. You don't have to grunt and groan to experience the beneficial effects. For most people, the easiest, most convenient type of exercise is walking. You can do it anywhere, at any time; it doesn't require any special equipment; and you can do it by yourself or with a friend. If you are afraid that it would be boring, take a portable cassette player along and listen to music. If the weather is bad, walk around a shopping mall—but don't stop to look in the windows until you've walked for thirty minutes.

Marie is a good example of someone who had difficulty establishing an exercise program. She was a fifty-five-year-old teacher who was a moderately depressed emotional eater. Although she found some satisfaction in her career, especially the professional writing she did, her relationships with others, including her physician husband, were not fulfilling. When I first mentioned the value of exercise, Marie was very negative. The word *exercise* immediately elicited memories of her hated high school gym class. After we discussed the differences, Marie recognized that there wouldn't be any "drill sergeant" teacher barking commands at her, or any seventeen-year-old cheerleaders to ridicule her efforts. She reluctantly agreed that exercise might be worthwhile if she could "find the time."

Fortunately, her daughter-in-law belonged to a health club and invited her to a water aerobics class. Marie surprised both of us—she loved it—and the effects on her mood were dramatic. She was noticeably less depressed. It's possible that some of the improvement came from regular social contact with her daughter-in-law, but her comments indicated that she felt better about herself because of the exercise. Despite her many achievements, Marie always had a sense of inadequacy about physical activity. Participation in the water aerobics was a major accomplishment, and she felt good about it.

If you have some doubts about exercise, here are some suggestions to help you get started:

1. Exercise is usually more fun if you do it with someone with whom you feel comfortable, *but . . .*
2. Avoid activities in which you compete with others.
3. Try activities that don't require special preparation or equipment.
4. Exercise for three thirty-minute periods each week. Establish a routine so you aren't confronted with decisions about when to exercise.
5. If your family and friends are supportive, make a public announcement about your exercise plans so that you will feel an obligation to follow through.
6. If you don't think you would like walking, try swimming, bicycling, or riding a stationary bicycle while watching television.
7. If you're having a hard time getting started, give yourself a nonedible reward the first few times.

Diet and Depression

You may be able to reduce your depressed moods by making some changes in your diet. In chapter 3 I described a study that implicated sugar and caffeine as a possible cause of depression for some people. Another study showed that eliminating refined sucrose and caffeine helped improve the mood of a group of clinically depressed subjects. After four weeks on a sucrose- and caffeine-free diet, half of the participants showed an improvement in depression on all the measures used, and 21 percent showed a partial improvement; only 29 percent showed no improvement. This was in contrast to a control group where 65 percent showed no improvement. The participants who improved and continued on the diet, maintained their improved mood at the three-month follow-up.[13] If you try this approach to treating depression, gradually taper your consumption of coffee, tea, and colas since an abrupt withdrawal may cause headaches. Keep track of your moods using the Emotional Eating Record. If you are sensitive to caffeine and sucrose, you should notice an effect on your mood in one to two weeks after you have eliminated them from your diet.

Finally, keep up your self-nurturing activities. Nurturing yourself is especially important if you tend to become depressed. Take a moment to review chapter 5 to make sure you have not let any of your self-nurturing attitudes or behaviors slide.

Anxiety and Eating

Anxiety-based emotional eating shows up in the most unexpected situations. One evening after coming home from a wedding shower for her cousin, Joanna found herself in the kitchen snacking. After a few minutes, she realized that she wasn't hungry; she was anxious. She stopped eating and started thinking about why. Later, in my office, she told me what triggered this episode.

Joanna was a successful woman. After earning her Ph.D., she went to work as an assistant professor of biology at a private university. When she grew dissatisfied with the limited opportunity for advancement, she started part time in an M.B.A. program. Seven years after completing the Ph.D. and two years after earning the M.B.A., she gave up her academic job and went to work for a Silicon Valley firm in the marketing department. Once inside the corporate world, she found it hard, as a female executive, to make her way up the corporate ladder. To be successful, she had to earn the trust and respect of her male bosses. Since it would have been inappropriate for her to go drinking with "the boys" after work, she did the next best thing: she played tennis, entered bike races, and went running with them. Although there were no written regulations about weight, a quick glance around the executive suites of the company would reveal that almost everyone appeared fit and slim. Her good relationships with the management and her hopes of future advancement in the company required that she keep her slim physique. But Joanna was short (5 feet, 3 inches) and, for much of her life, chubby (135 pounds). In order to keep her weight in the range of 105 to 110 pounds, she ate rice cakes for lunch, skinned chicken breasts for dinner, and celery stalks and carrots for snacks and used her Stairmaster daily. The slender physique, the long hours at work, and the carefully nurtured relationships with male colleagues paid off. After eight years with the company, she was appointed vice-president for research and development. Joanna had arrived. She had a six-figure salary, a house in the hills, and a Mercedes in the garage.

Joanna could have been the female version of Horatio Alger. She grew up in the Midwest, the fourth of six children. Her father, a marginally successful appliance repairman, was able to provide his family with an adequate standard of living, although Joanna's mother had to be very thrifty. Joanna was eleven when her father died, and life became considerably more difficult.

Understanding this history helped Joanna to understand her unusual episode of emotional eating. The wedding shower for Tiffany, Joanna's twenty-nine-year-old cousin, brought back anxiety-provoking memories. Unlike Joanna, Tiffany had not succeeded in escaping her blue-collar background. At the shower, Joanna met Tiffany's friends and watched as they played party games. She felt uneasy, especially around the table laden with cake, Ho Hos, Ding Dongs, and bite-sized Milky Ways. She had one piece of cake and left the party early. When she got home, she finished off a container of yogurt, made herself a sandwich, and started on a bag of cookies. Joanna felt empty inside. She wasn't nervous or tense, but she needed to feel full, even though she knew that she wasn't hungry. Inside, a voice was telling her to stop eating, but there was a stronger desire to feel full. Joanna had grown comfortable in her upper-income, achievement-oriented world, and Tiffany's shower brought back memories and fears from her less secure childhood. Especially the party games and packaged snacks reminded her of the world that she had escaped. The resulting anxiety could be soothed only by eating. Feeling full would make the vague, free-floating anxiety go away. Once she recognized that she was anxious, not hungry, and then identified the source of the anxiety, the urge to eat stopped.

Anxiety and Eating

Of all the emotions, anxiety has the longest history of being linked to eating. In a classic paper, Harold Kaplan and Helen Singer Kaplan reviewed dozens of psychoanalytic case studies and discussion articles. Based on these writings, they compiled a lengthy list of unconscious meanings of overeating and obesity. Although some were a bit fanciful (overeating may symbolically represent an "alimentary orgasm"), many were similar to commonly accepted explanations for overeating. For example, overeating was described as a diversion from monotony or as a means of rewarding oneself for accomplishment of a task. Confronted with the list of possible conflicts that could produce emotional eating, the authors concluded that *any* emotional conflict can cause anxiety. They suggested that eating is physiologically incompatible with anxiety and therefore, intense anxiety is reduced by eating.[1]

Since this 1957 review, several studies have shown that the link between anxiety and eating is not as simple as the Kaplans suggested. Several laboratory studies, including one that I conducted, failed to find a relationship between anxiety and eating.[2] Joyce Slochower, a psychologist, suggested that in many of the studies (including mine), there was a clear source of anxiety; the subjects in the study knew what was making them stressed. She demonstrated that for overweight college students, anxiety provokes eating only when it is diffuse or free floating.[3] In other words, if you are anxious because you are going for a job interview in two hours, you can identify the source of the anxiety and are not as likely to eat. But if you are in a situation like Joanna's where you are uneasy but can't identify what is making you anxious, you are more likely to eat. In another study, Dr. Slochower told some of the overweight participants that they could control their anxiety state by using a simple breathing exercise. Although none of the participants used this exercise, just thinking that they could control their anxiety was enough to reduce their eating.[4] The results of these studies demonstrate that when you know what is causing the anxiety and feel that you will be able to control it, you won't need to eat. These findings have direct implications for controlling anxious eating. Your goals should be to identify the source of your anxiety and then develop techniques for reducing the anxiety without eating.

Identifying the Source of Anxiety

The cognitive therapy approach is as useful for anxiety as it was for depression. Recall that cognitive therapy is based on the premise that it is the thoughts we have about an event that cause the emotion rather than the event itself. In the usual sequence, an event is an antecedent, which is followed by a thought, which provokes an emotion (A-T-E). For anxiety, the antecedent is usually an upcoming event; the thought typically is worry about anticipated danger or harm. Thinking about the danger or harm associated with the upcoming event elicits feelings of anxiety. For example, many people become anxious when they have to give a talk to a group of people. This is the antecedent. If you're one of them, you may think something like, "What happens if I lose my train of thought? I'll stand there speechless. I'll get so nervous that I'll sweat and shake, and everyone will know I don't know what I'm talking about. I'll make a complete fool of myself." These thoughts produce anxiety, the emotion.

Using the A-T-E format, I had Joanna consider what happened before she started on the yogurt, sandwich, and cookies binge. This is the sequence she identified:

Antecedent: *Tiffany's Wedding Shower*

Thought(s): *1. If I'm not careful, I'll gain weight or screw up at work. I could lose everything and end up like Tiffany and her friends,*

2. I'm really a fat, poor kid, not a slender executive

3. I shouldn't be so uncomfortable around Tiffany's friends.

Emotion: *Anxiety*

Go back to your Emotional Eating Record and find the last instance of eating triggered by anxiety. Try to recall where you were and what was going on so that you can identify the antecedent. If you are not sure, write in your best guess(es) in the space below; then see if you can identify the thought(s) that elicited the emotion, and write them in also:

Antecedent:_____

Thought(s):_____

_____

_____

Emotion: *Anxiety*_____

Learning to identify the A-T-E sequences that trigger anxious eating is important to establish control. To practice, review your Emotional Eating Record again to find another example of anxious eating and find the thought that elicited the anxiety:

Antecedent:_____

Thought(s):_____

_____

_____

Emotion: *Anxiety*_____

If you've succeeded in identifying some of the thoughts that make you anxious, you may recognize that they are not entirely rational. When you challenge the distortions in your thinking, you will be less anxious, and not feel the need to eat. Using Dr. Burns's list (see pp. 95–97), I asked Joanna to identify the type of twisted thinking implicit in each of her anxiety-provoking thoughts and to provide a rational response to substitute for the twisted thought:

Date *Friday* Time *9:00* P.M. Antecedent *Tiffany's Wedding Shower*

Thought	Type of Twisted Thinking	Rational Response
1. *I'll screw-up and gain weight. I'll lose every-thing.*	*Fortune telling*	*I am doing well. There is no reason to think I'm going to lose everything.*
2. *I'm really a poor, fat kid.*	*Labeling*	*Even if I gain weight or lose my job, it's not likely to be permanent.*
3. *I should not be uncomfortable around Tiffany's friends*	*Should statement*	*It's okay if I feel a little uncomfort-able. I don't have to enjoy being social all the time*

With anxiety, one of the most common types of twisted thinking is fortune telling (a subpart of distortion 5). Usually this takes the form of predicting that some type of disaster is imminent. Joanna's thought that she would gain weight or "screw up" and lose everything that she had worked so hard to accomplish is fortune telling because she has no factual basis for this prediction. Despite her discomfort at the party, all the evidence suggests that she is doing well at her job and there is no reason to doubt that she will be able to continue her current standard of living. It is likely that there is also labeling (distortion 9) implicit in her thoughts. Despite her obvious successes, she sees herself as an imposter. She still labels herself as a fat kid from a poor family. A label suggests a permanent condition. This is irrational because even if she gained weight or lost her job, it is quite likely that she could get a new job and lose weight again.

Joanna's third thought about being uncomfortable around Tiffany's friends is a classic *should* statement (distortion 8). There is no edict or commandment that requires anyone to enjoy the company of anyone else. When I asked Joanna about the party, she said she felt awkward because she didn't want to feel as if she was bragging about her life-style, so she was careful about what she discussed with Tiffany's friends. Since she didn't know them well and felt she had to censor what she said to them, it was not surprising that she was uncomfortable. When Joanna recognized the distortions in her thinking and was able to counter them with more logical thoughts, she stopped being anxious and lost the urge to eat.

Now it's your turn. For the first A-T-E sequence you completed above, write in the thought, the type of illogical thinking implicit in the thought, and a more rational response.

Date _____ Time _____ Antecedent _____

Thought	Type of Twisted Thinking	Rational Response
_____	_____	_____
_____	_____	_____
_____	_____	_____
_____	_____	_____

Now repeat this procedure for the second A-T-E sequence.

Date _____ Time _____ Antecedent _____

Thought	Type of Twisted Thinking	Rational Response
_____	_____	_____
_____	_____	_____
_____	_____	_____
_____	_____	_____

Confronted with all of these blank spaces to fill in, I won't blame you if you feel a bit overwhelmed. Try not to get anxious about having to fill in charts for the rest of your life (that would be fortune telling—distortion 5). It is necessary to have you do all of this record keeping now, to make the automatic thought processes become less automatic. Once you are in the habit of stopping to examine your thoughts when you start to feel anxious and get the urge to snack, you will be able to use this process without all the paperwork.

Anxiety-Control Techniques

Identifying and correcting illogical thinking will greatly reduce anxiety. So will several other methods. Review these methods, and try one or more while continuing to work on your thinking.

Exposure

In a *Newsweek* essay, television producer Ken Hecht described how he reduced his weight from 315 to 187 pounds. Although he makes the mistake of assuming that what worked for him will work for every other obese person, the "cold turkey" approach he described could be useful for other anxious eaters: "I wanted to just sit there and see if the nightmarish anxiety I so feared would in fact total me. So I sat and felt god-awful and eventually felt feelings of self-loathing and disgust and worthlessness. And finally the panicky desire to eat passed. It lasted less than 30 minutes."[5] He admits that it wasn't his last binge, but knowing that he could cope with the anxiety allowed him to feel good about himself and, over time, give up anxious eating.

Confronting your anxieties directly and waiting for the unpleasantness to pass is the basis for an approach called flooding or exposure, which some behavior therapists use. David Barlow and Jerome Cerny reviewed a large body of research on this type of treatment and concluded that "prolonged exposure to a fearful situation does facilitate the elimination of fearful and panic-like responses to those fearful situations."[6]

Direct confrontation of fears is not for everyone. You have to be able to identify the source of the anxiety so that you can expose yourself to it, and you have to prepare yourself for a prolonged exposure to the stimulus; a brief exposure does not help. Like Ken Hecht, you have to be willing to keep at it until the stimulus loses its power over you. Exposure is one of the least time-consuming methods of anxiety reduction, and although the prospect of continuous confrontation of a feared stimulus or situation may seem horrible, this approach can work.

Paradoxical Intention

Anxiety usually involves an expectation of something bad happening. The emotional arousal occurs as you worry and try to avoid whatever it is. Paradoxical intention, another means of confronting unrealistic anxieties, is useful when you are anxious about something that you will do or not do.[7]

Jennifer, a college student, told me that she was afraid of

fainting while sitting in class. As she discussed her fears, she became increasingly anxious. I asked her to go to class and try to faint. Although she was skeptical, she reluctantly agreed to try. Despite her best efforts, Jennifer could not make herself faint. After class, the anxiety was gone. She was laughing as she told me how silly she felt trying unsuccessfully to faint.

Therapists have used this technique with other anxieties like fear of being unable to get an erection when sexually aroused, fear of going crazy, and fear of being unable to get to sleep. George Clum, a psychologist, points out that you can't lose with this approach. If, like Jennifer, you try to make the feared event happen and it doesn't happen, you have learned that your fear was unfounded. If it does happen, you learn that the consequences are not nearly as bad as you had expected, and you have had some practice coping with them.[8]

The next time you find yourself anxiously eating, see if you can identify the source of your anxiety. If it is something outside yourself that you are afraid of, exposure should be helpful. If you are anxious about something you might do, try to make it happen. Both exposure and paradoxical intention should reduce anxiety and increase your sense of control.

Distraction

If you are feeling anxious and have the urge to eat but cannot identify the source of the anxiety, distraction techniques should be helpful. You've probably had some experience with this technique already. Perhaps you were anxiously brooding about an upcoming event when the telephone rang. You got involved in a conversation with a friend and only later remembered what it was that you were so anxious about. Instead of leaving distraction to chance, you can plan easily accessible distractions that you can use when you feel the emotional eating urge coming on.

David Burns suggests carrying around a small puzzle that requires concentration and manipulation.[9] A Rubik's Cube on a key chain is ideal, but any other small puzzle that engages your interest would work. Put aside a favorite book or magazine to read when you need to be distracted, or save an ongoing activity or hobby for these times. Esther, a forty-eight-year-old teacher, found herself anxiously snacking after dinner. I knew from our previous conversations that she had several years' worth of photographs that she wanted to organize and put in albums when she had the time. Since looking at photos was a pleasantly distracting activity, I encouraged her to leave the album and a small stack of photos on a corner of her desk in the family room. Several times a week in the evenings, when she felt the urge to snack, she worked on her album. She became engrossed in the pictures and positioning them in the album. Most of the time, the urge to snack passed after a few minutes.

Some anxious people reject the suggestion of distracting themselves because they are afraid that they won't be able to concentrate on a book or activity. This kind of thinking is emotional reasoning (distortion 7). You assume that because you are anxious and can feel the physiological arousal, you won't be able to concentrate, read, or do anything other than worry. This may not be true. Before you dismiss the idea, try a distracting activity, and see if it doesn't reduce your anxiety.

Relaxation

More than fifty years ago, Edmund Jacobson demonstrated that relaxation exercises decrease pulse rate and blood pressure.[10] Since then, psychologists have been using relaxation exercises with their patients to decrease anxiety. The specific method you use to teach yourself to relax—meditation, biofeedback, progressive muscle relaxation, or breathing exercises—is not important. What is important is that you learn this skill so that when you are anxious and feel the urge to eat, you can relax easily.

Progressive muscle relaxation is comprised of simple, easily learned exercises intended to relax the muscles throughout the body. Dr. Jacobson noticed that even when people were involved in a leisure activity or lying down, their muscles were still contracted. In progressive muscle relaxation, you alternately tense and relax different groups of muscles. By tensing the muscles, you will be able to contrast the feeling of muscle tension with the feeling when your muscles are relaxed. This process will help you recognize when your muscles are tensed so that you can tune in to that muscle group and relax it. With practice, you will be able to relax your muscles whenever you start to feel tense.

To learn muscle relaxation, plan on daily practice sessions lasting about a half-hour. Find a time when you won't be interrupted by your children, the telephone, the doorbell, or other distractions. Sit in a comfortable chair or sofa, and loosen any tight clothing or jewelry.

Now focus your attention on a group of muscles. Contract those muscles so you can experience them being tensed, and then relax them so that you can feel the contrast between tension and relaxation. Many people experience a sense of warmth or heaviness in the muscles as they become more relaxed. After one muscle group is relaxed, move on to the next group, until you have relaxed all the muscles in your body.

Read the following instructions several times to get a sense of the procedure. You can also make a tape recording of yourself slowly reading the instructions and play the tape during your practice sessions.

Begin by sitting back in a comfortable chair with your arms at your sides, your hands on your lap, and your feet flat on the floor. Keep your eyes closed throughout the exercise. Whey you're feeling comfortable, take two or three slow, deep breaths, noticing the passage of air into and out of your lungs and diaphragm. Now hold out your right arm and make a hard fist with your right hand. Notice the tension in your fist as you tighten it. After 5 to 10 seconds of concentrating on the tension, relax your hand. Undo the fist and notice how the tension recedes and sensations of relaxation and comfort take its place. Focus on the difference between the tension and the relaxation. After about 15 to 20 seconds, make a fist of your right hand again, study the tension for 5 to 10 seconds, and relax. Feel the relaxation and warmth. After 15 to 20 seconds, repeat the procedure, this time with your left hand. Be sure to focus only on the muscle group you're tensing and relaxing, and try not to tense the rest of your body at the same time.[11]

Repeat this sequence for additional muscle groups. For each, tense the muscles, and concentrate on the tension for five to ten seconds; then release the tension and focus on the difference between tension and relaxation for fifteen to twenty seconds. This tense-hold-release-relax sequence is repeated a second time before moving on to the next muscle group. The muscle groups and the tensing action are listed below:

1. Right hand: Make a fist
2. Left hand: Make a fist.
3. Right arm: Bend at the elbow; tighten biceps muscle.
4. Left arm: Bend at the elbow; tighten biceps muscle.
5. Right arm: Stretch outward; tighten triceps muscle.
6. Left arm: Stretch outward; tighten triceps muscle.
7. Shoulders: Hunch shoulders forward.
8. Neck: Head forward, push chin into your chest.
9. Mouth: Open wide.
10. Tongue: Push upward against the roof of the mouth.
11. Eyes: Close tightly.
12. Forehead: Raise eyebrows as high as possible.
13. Chest: Take a deep breath, hold it, and slowly exhale.

14. Back: Arch your back, and push your chest out. (Skip this muscle group if you have back problems.)
15. Buttocks: Contract muscles by pushing against the chair.
16. Stomach: Pull in stomach.
17. Thighs: Straighten legs, and lift them a few inches off the floor.
18. Calves: Feet on the floor, point toes toward your head.
19. Feet: Push your toes down against the bottom of your shoes.

Throughout the session, pause after every several muscle groups to see if any tension has returned to the muscles already relaxed. If this has happened, go back and relax those muscles again. When you finish the sequence, sit quietly enjoying the relaxed feeling. Pick a favorite relaxing scene and daydream about it. When I use relaxation exercises, I like to visualize myself lying on a beach and listening to the ocean, with the warmth of the sun on my back. Being able to picture the sights and sensations of a pleasant scene vividly is especially useful if you find your mind wandering back to chores that you have to do or other anxiety-producing thoughts.

Perhaps you are feeling a little overwhelmed by the sequence of muscle groups to be relaxed. Don't make yourself anxious over the relaxation exercises. If you forget one muscle group or do them out of sequence, it's no calamity. By practicing daily, you'll find that the process becomes easier. After two weeks, it's likely that you'll be able to relax yourself in a few minutes.

Regardless of whether you use progressive muscle relaxation, exposure, paradoxical intention, or distraction, you should also continue to work on the twisted thoughts that produce the anxiety. As you continue to do this, understand what is making you anxious, and see that you have some control over your anxiety, the need to use food as a tranquilizer will decrease.

Boredom, Loneliness, and Eating

Eating when bored or lonely are the most common types of emotional eating regardless of weight. One survey found that 28 percent of normal-weight people admitted eating when bored or lonely. Among successful dieters who had maintained their weight loss for one year, 36 percent still ate when lonely or bored.[1] Although boredom and loneliness are often experienced together, it is possible to be bored and not lonely, or lonely and not bored. For the sake of clarity, we'll consider them separately.

Boredom

Shawn Stinson, a graduate student working under my supervision, studied the effects of boredom on eating. The college students who participated in this study were offered roast beef sandwiches so that hunger would not affect the results. Then half of the subjects were given a boring task—they sat alone in a small, windowless room for twenty-five minutes and wrote the letters "cd" over and over again. The other subjects were asked to write imaginative stories based on dramatic pictures they were shown. After he finished giving the instructions, the experimenter casually emptied a box of Wheat Thins into a bowl and invited the subject to help himself. Both overweight and normal-weight subjects in the boring task ate more than those in the more interesting task.[2]

Eating can alleviate boredom. In fact, sometimes it may be the only legitimate alternative to a boring activity. In some offices, it's acceptable to stop working on a boring task at 10:30 in the morning to have coffee and a doughnut. There would be problems, however, if you stopped working to read a magazine or play cards for ten minutes. Even if the bored eater does not view cooking as a hobby or interest, often he or she will choose a food that requires some preparation. For example, the bored eater may make brownies rather than eat store-bought cookies, or make a ritual out of popping popcorn and eating it. Sometimes preparing the food can be as useful in combating the boredom as eating it.

Eating when bored is a common experience for many people, regardless of weight. For a few people, bored eating becomes a daily routine, which can lead to weight gain or bulimia. Amy, a twenty-year-old college junior, came to see me at her parents' insistence after they discovered that she was making herself throw up.

Amy had everything going for her. She grew up in the ideal family. Her father was a college physics professor; her mother was a teacher; her older brother and sister were both college graduates. Amy seemed to be headed in the same direction. She was a cheerleader and a straight A student in high school. After graduating, she went to a prestigious midwestern university. But she found the academic pressure too demanding and felt out of place in the sorority-oriented social environment. After one semester on academic probation and a second semester with improved grades, she came home to attend the small college where her father taught. Amy did well in her classes and enjoyed being back with many of her high school friends.

The problem with emotional eating started the following year when her father took a sabbatical and moved across the country to teach at another university. Amy went with her parents and once again found herself out of place. She was doing well in the four courses she was taking, lived in an apartment with two roommates, and frequently saw her parents. But there wasn't enough for Amy to do, especially in the afternoons when she came home from classes. Her typical pattern was to return to her apartment at about 3:30 and either turn on the television or try to study. After a few minutes, she would think about other things she'd rather be doing and get up and start to snack. After she had finished several candy bars or cookies, she had the sensation of fullness in her stomach combined with guilt about having blown her diet. The negative thoughts about gaining weight continued until she made herself vomit. She felt badly about throwing up and the possibility of gaining weight, yet her afternoon snacks were important to her. Although she usually had a good lunch, in her afternoon classes she would daydream about what she would eat when she got home.

As Amy described her daily routine, there was little doubt that she was bored and used her afternoon snacks as an activity to relieve the boredom. She saw herself as having few alternatives. She knew that in three months her father's sabbatical would be over, and the family would return home. She felt that making friends, finding a job, or starting any new activity was pointless since she would be leaving soon. We worked on finding self-nurturing behaviors that she could substitute for her afternoon snacks. Although she had some concerns about not fitting in, she joined a coed intramural volleyball team that practiced in the late afternoons. Episodes of bored eating and self-induced vomiting decreased markedly.

Amy's bored eating was easy to identify. She had a large block of time with little to do so she ate. If you lead a busy life, there may be few, if any, periods when you have nothing to do. Even if you're busy all the time, you may still eat when bored. When an activity is not interesting or challenging, boredom results. The subjects in Shawn Stinson's boredom study were busy writing letters on sheets of paper. Despite their activity, they became bored and ate. You may find it more difficult to identify this type of bored eating because you are busy so it isn't obvious that you are feeling bored.

Unlike anxiety or anger, which are characterized by strong physiological arousal, boredom is usually associated with little or no physiological arousal. Since your body is not giving you any cues, it may be hard to identify when you are bored; you just know that you are eating when you aren't hungry. If you are not sure if you're a bored eater, check your Emotional Eating Record for clues. Is there one time period in which you find frequent emotional eating? Maybe your daily routine has a period that doesn't provide enough stimulation. Do certain foods that require preparation or involve little rituals reappear on the record? You may use these food activities to avoid boredom. In the Emotion column, do you find question marks or blank spaces? Pay attention to your thoughts. Even if you are busy doing something, does your mind wander? Do you tend to think about other things that you would rather be doing? Look over your Emotional Eating Record to see if you can identify eating associated with boredom.

Controlling Bored Eating

It is not difficult to control bored eating, although it will take some planning. First review your Emotional Eating Record to determine if the bored eating is the result of having nothing to do or of doing an activity that doesn't interest you. For bored eating when there is nothing to do, identify the times and places where this is most likely to occur. Then you can plan to have an activity that will be involving for that time or place. Go back to chapter 5, and review your responses to the section on self-nurturing behaviors. You can use the same activities that you chose for self-nurturance. Just make sure that they do not require a great deal of preparation or equipment. It is likely that you will have to make a conscious effort to plan these activities. For example, if you are a student who is bored in the late afternoon and you don't want to do your homework until after dinner, work on a hobby when you get home. Before you leave in the morning, make sure you put the hobby materials out so that it will be easy to get started as soon as you return home.

If you find that most of your bored eating occurs when you are doing tasks that you find uninteresting and you do not have the option of doing something more interesting, you will have to alter your environment to make eating less likely. Usually this means doing the boring task someplace where it is difficult to eat. For example, Amber, a thirty-nine-year-old pharmaceutical firm representative, found herself eating while filling out the report forms for each of the calls she made during the day. Her usual pattern was to come home in the late afternoon, set up the typewriter on the kitchen table, and work on the forms. After eleven years with the same company, she found this task to be tedious, but there was no way of avoiding it. As she worked on the reports she would find her mind wandering. Sometimes when she was looking for a word to express a thought and she was stumped, she'd get up and browse through the refrigerator to find something to eat. She wasn't hungry, but she was bored, and eating provided an easy alternative to struggling with her reports. Also, she knew that if she read the newspaper or tried to use another activity as a diversion, there was a risk that she would get involved in the new activity and not finish her reports. On the other hand, if she got up, looked in the refrigerator, and spent a few minutes eating what she found, the whole sequence would take less than ten minutes before she would go back to report writing. Usually this bored-browse-eat sequence was repeated three or four times before the afternoon's reports were completed.

For Amber, it was relatively easy to decrease the frequency of bored eating. Most days, she was able to complete some of her reports while waiting in doctors' offices for her next appointment. Since there wasn't any food in the waiting rooms, she didn't eat while working on the reports. Usually she had a few reports left to do at the end of the day. If the weather was good, she'd stop at a park near her home and do some of the work before going home. When she had to do reports at home, she took the work into the bedroom. Although she still had access to the refrigerator, the need to walk down the hall and through the family room to get to the kitchen gave her the opportunity to recognize that she was bored, not hungry. Once she became aware that she was bored, she was able to substitute another brief activity—water the plants, file her nails, unload the dishwasher, or clean the parakeet's cage. Any of these activities provided a brief diversion from the boring task without having to eat.

In many ways bored eating is the most straightforward type of emotional eating to control. Once you have identified the situations where bored eating is most likely you have two possible solutions to the problem. The first is to find more interesting activities. If this is impossible because you are obligated to do a boring task, then try to do it someplace where food is not available.

Loneliness

Author Kim Chernin confesses:

> But now suddenly, for the first time in my life, I realized that what I was feeling was not hunger at all. I was restless, that was true; I had awakened feeling lonely, I was sad at being alone in the house. . . . What I wanted from food was companionship, comfort, reassurance, a sense of warmth and well-being that was hard for me to find in my own life, even in my own home.[3]

Does this sound familiar? Do you use food to cope with loneliness? Before considering its effects on your eating, it would be helpful to get an objective measure of your experience of loneliness. Asking, "Are you lonely?" may not be sufficient. There is frequently a stigma associated with loneliness. Given the value that we place on being popular and outgoing, it can be difficult or embarrassing to recognize when you don't have very many relationships or that the relationships that you do have are superficial or unsatisfying. As a result, some people may not be aware that they are lonely or may incorrectly label their loneliness.[4] Other problems, like alcohol abuse, may mask the distress a person feels due to a lack of close relationships. Since recognizing loneliness is not always straightforward, it would help to complete the Revised UCLA Loneliness Scale (Table 9–1). It will give you an objective measure of your loneliness and allow you to compare your score with norms for other groups.

To score the scale, reverse the scores for the items with an asterisk (items 1, 4, 5, 6, 9, 10, 15, 16, 19, and 20): a score of 1 is changed to 4, 2 becomes 3, 3 becomes 2, and 4 becomes 1. Then add up the sum of the scores on all twenty items. Compare your score with the norms presented in Table 9–2 and then review your Emotional Eating Record. If you find that your Loneliness score is high and you have few instances of

TABLE 9-1

Revised UCLA Loneliness Scale

Directions: Indicate how often you feel the way described in each of the following statements. Circle one number for each.

Statement	Never	Rarely	Some-times	Often
1 I feel in tune with the people around me.*	1	2	3	4
2 I lack companionship	1	2	3	4
3 There is no one I can turn to	1	2	3	4
4 I do not feel alone*	1	2	3	4
5 I feel part of a group of friends*	1	2	3	4
6 I have a lot in common with the people around me*	1	2	3	4
7 I am no longer close to anyone	1	2	3	4
8 My interests and ideas are not shared by those around me	1	2	3	4
9 I am an outgoing person*	1	2	3	4
10 There are people I feel close to*	1	2	3	4
11 I feel left out	1	2	3	4
12 My social relationships are superficial	1	2	3	4
13 No one really knows me well	1	2	3	4
14 I feel isolated from others	1	2	3	4
15 I can find companionship when I want it*	1	2	3	4
16 There are people who really understand me*	1	2	3	4
17 I am unhappy being so withdrawn	1	2	3	4

TABLE 9 – 1 (continued)

Statement	Never	Rarely	Some-times	Often
18 People are around me but not with me	1	2	3	4
19 There are people I can talk to*	1	2	3	4
20 There are people I can turn to*	1	2	3	4

Source: K. Russell, L. A. Peplau, and C. E. Cutrona, The Revised UCLA Loneliness Scale: Concurrent and discriminant validity evidence, *Journal of Personality and Social Psychology* 39 (1980): 472–480. © 1980 by the American Psychological Association. Reprinted by permission.

loneliness in the Emotions column on the records, consider the possibility that you may have not recognized when you were feeling lonely and eating. Paying particular attention to blank spaces or question marks, try to recall the circumstances and your thoughts to determine if loneliness was triggering your emotional eating.

In a study using the Revised UCLA Loneliness Scale, researchers found that obese women had significantly higher

TABLE 9 – 2
Norms for the Revised UCLA Loneliness Scale

Women		Men	
Score	Percentile	Score	Percentile
26	16	26	16
36	50	37	50
46	84	48	84
56	98	59	98

loneliness scores (the average was 42) than nonobese women. There was no difference for men. The researchers speculate that for women, eating in response to loneliness may cause weight gains. Being overweight results in feelings of self-consciousness, social withdrawal, and further loneliness, which cause additional eating.[5]

Loneliness and Eating

Why is loneliness associated with eating? Think for a minute about how it feels to be lonely. What terms would you use to describe the feeling? Psychologist Robert S. Weiss, who has done some of the most influential research on loneliness, has provided a description that captures the essence of the experience: "a feeling of inner ache and almost intolerable restlessness."[6] In the same way that eating can tranquilize the unpleasantness of anxiety, it may also reduce the inner ache and restlessness of loneliness.

Think about the relationship between your feelings of loneliness and eating. If you use eating to compensate for a lack of meaningful contact with others, does it ultimately make you feel worse? In addition to weight gain, there may be feelings of shame and guilt, which make you less comfortable being close to others. The case of Sam, a thirty-eight-year-old bachelor, illustrates the vicious circle of eating to compensate for loneliness resulting in decreased social contact.

Sam had a difficult childhood. As the youngest of three sons, he was his macho father's last hope of producing a "warrior" for a son. But Sam was no more competitive or aggressive than his two older brothers. The combination of his father's frequently expressed disappointment and his mother's overprotectiveness resulted in Sam's being a shy, socially awkward child. Being shy as a child is not uncommon. Even if relationships are fewer in number and slower to develop, it is not necessary for a shy child to become a lonely adult.

Going into junior high school, Sam was a quiet, tall, thin kid with a few friends and no signs of emotional eating. But his few friends went to a different junior high, leaving Sam feeling isolated in an unfriendly environment. His tendency to withdraw became a focus of conflict between his parents. His mother became more protective in proportion to his father's unsympathetic attempts to "make a man" of Sam by forcing him into situations where he felt uncomfortable. Sam grew increasingly isolated.

As an adult, Sam worked for the family business and lived by himself, although he frequently went to his parents' home for dinner. Besides his family, his social contacts were limited to occasional chats with his neighbor when they were both out doing yard work and his work with the youth soccer league. Although he envied married couples, it was years since he had had a date. Sam, who now weighed over 230 pounds, admitted in his first session that he was very lonely.

Sam's Emotional Eating Record showed that he was frequently lonely, especially in the evenings and on weekends, and that he consoled himself with food. Usually his lonely eating was accompanied by wistful thoughts of the family life that he felt he would never have. Like Kim Chernin, he used food for "companionship, comfort, reassurance, a sense of warmth and well-being." One of the most important goals of therapy was to help Sam develop relationships.

Developing Relationships with People Instead of Food

Many lonely people, like Sam, have few social contacts. They are truly isolated from others. The majority of lonely individuals, however, are not lacking in contact with others. They may spend most of the day interacting at work, shopping, saying "hi" to the neighbors, and so on, but the quality of the interactions is superficial. Although they are around other people, they do not get most of the satisfactions of relationships.

If you are lonely, the first step is to decide whether you need more relationships or a deepening of the relationships you already have. Following the program developed by Jeffrey Young, I will describe methods for increasing the number of your social contacts and then methods for increasing the caring and intimacy of relationships.[7]

Increasing Social Contacts

Frequently socially isolated people have negative beliefs that prevent them from forming new relationships. On the basis of one or more unhappy experiences with previous relationships, they conclude that they have a flaw (e.g., "I'm unlovable") that ensures that any attempt to be close to another person is doomed to fail. If you are thinking, "That sounds like twisted thinking," congratulations; you've got the idea. If not, recall from chapter 7 that one form of twisted thinking is labeling. Thus, rather than focus on what caused the bad experience, you attach a label to yourself. For example, after a romantic relationship ends, you may conclude that you are an unlovable person. A second type of twisted thinking that is implicit in many instances of loneliness is fortune telling. Many lonely people project into the future and conclude that some relationships in the past did not work, so no future relationship will work. Since you are unlovable and all relationships are doomed to failure, there is no point in trying to get close to anyone. Thus, you don't do anything to meet people or to deepen relationships with people whom you already know.

Acting on the basis of these twisted thoughts ensures that you will continue to be lonely.

Dr. Young describes several other themes that are typical in the thinking of lonely people. One pattern often occurs following the end of a relationship—say, a divorce or when a friend stops calling. The lonely person will accept *all* of the responsibility for the end of the relationship. This is a type of twisted thinking called personalization. The reality is that when a relationship ends, usually it isn't the fault of one person. People change with the passage of time, but they don't always change in the same way. Other times when a relationship gets started, neither partner sees the areas of incompatibility, or both people recognize differences but incorrectly assume that they are unimportant. This is the romantic, but frequently, unrealistic, idea that "love will conquer all." Even if you are convinced that the failure of a relationship was entirely your fault, it doesn't make sense to withdraw from other relationships. The only chance you have of correcting the flaw is by establishing new relationships and trying to change. Withdrawing, suffering from loneliness, and then eating to cope with loneliness is unlikely to improve future relationships.

Some lonely people have unrealistic expectations about what constitutes a worthwhile relationship. This is a variation of the *should* statement. In order for a relationship to be meaningful, it *should* include sharing of all intimate secrets, *should* last for a lifetime, *should* never have disagreements about important issues, and so on. While it is nice to have relationships that meet these various requirements, it is perfectly acceptable to have relationships that are short term, in which some topics are not discussed or revolve around a single activity like playing softball or going to concerts. Some relationships may be valuable though temporary. For example, if you move to a new city, you could join a newcomers' club, recognizing that once you have developed a network of friends, you are likely to be less interested in maintaining many of the relationships from the club. Neglecting potential friendships because they would not measure up to an arbitrary standard is likely to result in loneliness.

Finally, some lonely people experience anxieties that keep them from interacting with others. Sam was usually afraid that if he initiated a conversation, he would be "bothering" the other person. If he did talk to someone, he worried that he would say something stupid or do something that would embarrass himself (fortune telling). His anxiety and self-consciousness made it difficult to be natural and enjoy socializing. When I pointed out that the other soccer league coaches seemed to enjoy talking to him, he attributed their acceptance of him to being polite (discounting the positive). When Sam corrected his twisted thinking, he was less anxious and more willing to try to make new friends.

Correcting twisted thinking about relationships is necessary but may not be sufficient to overcome loneliness. Once your thoughts and expectations about relationships are rational, you may discover that you lack one or two skills that make socializing go smoothly. These are not character flaws or pervasive personality problems but, rather, specific skills that you can learn. For example, when you are introduced to someone at a social gathering, do you let the other person do most of the talking and just respond by nodding and agreeing? Or maybe you go to the other extreme and dominate the conversation or tell too much about yourself before the other person is comfortable with you. Several books can be helpful in learning social skills.[8]

Deepening Relationships

After you have learned to make social contacts or if this has never been a problem for you, you may still feel lonely because your relationships rarely progress beyond casual friendships. Again, check your thinking to determine if there are illogical thoughts that prevent the deepening of relationships.

As most relationships deepen, the conversations usually move beyond discussions of sports, office politics, movies, and the weather to talk about more personal topics. It takes some time before enough trust develops so that you can be comfortable revealing problems or feelings that might make you feel vulnerable if they became common knowledge. Most lonely people are torn: they would like to be able to share their inner feelings with someone but fear that if they make a mistake or misjudge the trustworthiness of a potential confidant, they will be seen as inadequate and ultimately will be rejected. Rather than risk these unpleasant outcomes, the lonely individual continues the friendship on a casual basis. Frequently, this choice is justified on the basis of a past experience. Thus, he or she will conclude, "You can't trust anyone" or that office politics prevents real friendships. This, of course, is overgeneralization. While it is true that some co-workers may not be sympathetic, it is unlikely that you can't trust anyone. You need to know when it is safe to share some of your private thoughts.

If you find that you are lonely despite having casual friends, the first step to decreasing loneliness is to identify one or two of your friends whom you would like to know better. You may feel that none of your current friends is suitable for a deeper relationship because none shares your political views, or they all have different hobbies, or some other difference. This type of objection suggests a *should* statement. The underlying belief is something like, "For me to be close to someone, he or she *should* have the same religious beliefs as I do." If you wait until you find someone who meets all of your shoulds, it is likely that you will remain lonely. It is more realistic for you to accept the differences and become closer based on interests that you do have in common.

Usually the process of deepening a relationship takes time. It typically starts with one of the casual friends testing the waters by offering some personal information. It is not necessary to reveal your deepest secrets; just take a little risk. Since close relationships involve sharing in both directions, you will want to give your friend the opportunity to share his or her experiences and to offer comments about the information you have provided. If your friend does not truly understand how you are feeling or even if he or she responds with an unsympathetic comment, don't blow it out of proportion (this would be magnification). Although it doesn't feel good to be misunderstood, the worst thing that is likely to happen is that you will decide to resume a casual friendship with this person and look elsewhere for a deeper relationship. Keep in mind that developing a meaningful relationship takes some time. The history of most close relationships includes downs as well as ups. The process of overcoming misunderstandings helps to develop the strong bond that makes the relationship worthwhile.

In both bored eating and lonely eating, food is used as a substitute for something missing—either interesting activities or satisfying relationships. In both, eating provides an easy, if temporary and ultimately unsatisfying, means of filling the void. It takes more effort to develop more stimulating activities to prevent boredom. It takes more effort and the participation of others to develop satisfying relationships that will dispel loneliness. Think of the effort as an investment in your emotional well-being that will pay dividends in reduced eating.

Anger and Eating

The relationship between anger and eating is reflected in some of the colloquial expressions we use to describe our angry feelings. When someone says something that you don't agree with, you may have difficulty "swallowing it." If they persist, you may describe yourself as "fed up," and if it gets bad enough, you may have a hard time "stomaching it"—to the point that you "spit it out" and say, "It makes me sick" or, if you are really upset, "I want to puke." Eventually, if you are persuaded that you have been wrong, you may have to "swallow" your pride and "eat" your words. Is it a coincidence that so many expressions about anger and conflict include terms that deal with eating?

Expressed Anger and Eating

There is ample evidence that for many people, anger is related to eating. For Vince, a forty-six-year-old bakery route salesman, the connection was unmistakable.

At his peak, Vince weighed 401 pounds. He joined Weight Watchers and became their star pupil as he got his weight down to 190. After several months, he became annoyed with the Weight Watchers leader; he had several arguments with her and watched his weight climb back up to 280. This was only the most recent of several dramatic weight losses followed by equally dramatic gains.

When he was in one of his weight-gain phases, Vince would snack in his truck between deliveries and help himself to candy bars and ice cream at the convenience stores he stocked each day. When he was losing weight, he never snacked, followed a strict diet, and exercised vigorously every day.

Vince was an angry man. He described himself as a "tough guy" when he was in the service in Vietnam. He had a black belt in karate, and as a young man, he enjoyed boxing, barroom brawls, and watching wrestling on television. Although it had been years since his last fight, he admitted with shame that he had been in a counseling group for abusive husbands. At work, he had a stormy relationship with his boss and two of the other salesmen. After a real or imagined slight, Vince would get into shouting matches, culminating in his boss's threatening to fire him. The boss backed down only because Vince outsold all the other salesmen.

In our sessions, Vince described a violent childhood. His father routinely got drunk and beat Vince, his mother, and his brother. Vince was either afraid or angry for much of his childhood. As a sixteen year old, he was able to intercede and stop one of his father's rages. From that point on, he was rarely afraid but frequently angry. For Vince, being big meant that he could take care of himself. As he was regaining weight from his low of 190 pounds, he recalled that at 190, "I was little. I felt exposed and vulnerable." Eating made Vince feel better. It ensured that he'd be big and would not need to be afraid. When he was angry, snack foods were like spinach for Popeye: they made him stronger.

In therapy, the childhood roots of Vince's anger became

apparent. His father provided a model; he showed Vince "how to do it" and demonstrated that aggression got you what you wanted. The father's physical abuse and verbal demeaning made Vince hypersensitive to any threat to his fragile self-esteem. When he was threatened, Vince became angry and ate.

Suppressed Anger and Eating

Although the relationship between the overt expression of anger and eating is apparent for people like Vince, most of the psychological theorizing has focused on the effects of suppressed anger on eating. *Suppressed anger* is one of those slippery psychological terms that everyone uses even though they don't always agree on its meaning. I think of suppressed anger as angry feelings that are experienced but not expressed directly.

Trudy, a forty-two-year-old divorced woman who weighed 225 pounds is a good example of the suppressed anger-eating relationship. At our first session, she smiled sweetly as she recounted a lengthy list of physical symptoms and unsuccessful visits to several doctors in a futile attempt to find relief. Despite her pleasant demeanor, it quickly became apparent that Trudy was an angry woman. Five years earlier, she had left her husband, an attorney who drank heavily and beat her, moving back to the small community where her parents lived. She described, still with a smile on her face, how her mother treated her "like a twelve year old" by constantly telling her what to do, how to feel, and what to eat. Trudy's mother expressed concern about Trudy's weight and frequently suggested diets. Over the years, her mother's guiding principle was, "Don't get angry; don't get sad; just put a smile on your face." Trudy dutifully complied.

One morning, Trudy appeared for her session without her

characteristic smile. With some encouragement, she acknowledged that she was angry with her doctor because he would
not show her a medical report that he had received from another doctor. She left his office without saying anything to
him, went home and slammed the door, had a little tantrum,
and started to "wander from pantry to cupboard and eat until
I was sick." She reported that the food made her feel calmer—a
significant realization for Trudy. It was the first time she con-
nected her bingeing with anger.

During the next few weeks, she started to recognize how she
was feeling when she was bingeing. She was angry! Usually it
was with her mother, but she was also angry with her father
and her ex-husband. Each week she would tell me about
binges that were cut short by recollections of episodes that
made her angry. For example, one day she caught herself eating peanuts, stopped and recognized the angry feelings, and
then asked herself, "What am I angry about?" Earlier that
afternoon in a telephone conversation, her mother had
abruptly changed the topic when Trudy described a disappointment at work. When we discussed these instances of
anger-related eating, we followed the antecedent-thought-
emotion format. After Trudy recognized that she was angry, it
was easy to find the antecedent—usually something her
mother said or did. It was more difficult to identify the thought
and decide if it was logical. Once she recognized the thought,
Trudy could plan what, if anything, she wanted to do about
her anger. Trudy decided to discuss her feelings with her
mother calmly. Each time Trudy brought the topic up, her
mother steadfastly insisted that Trudy was wrong or was exaggerating. Following each attempt, Trudy felt more frustrated and angry. Finally, Trudy was convinced that she would
not be able to discuss her angry feelings with her mother. Since
she did not like her job and there was nothing else keeping her,
Trudy decided to move to a new town.

Angry Eating versus Angry Not Eating

Many psychological theorists have speculated about the link between anger and eating or anger and not eating. Usually eating or refusing to eat is seen as a means for women to cope with suppressed anger that they cannot express directly. From a feminist perspective, psychotherapist Susie Orbach describes how anger and eating are related for women:

> We are raised to be demure and accept what we are given with no complaints. We all learn how little girls are made of sugar and spice and all things nice. So we try hard not to show our anger or even feel it ourselves. When we rebel and show dissatisfaction we learn we are nasty and greedy. . . . It is not surprising, therefore, to find that for many women, the unconscious motivation behind the weight gain is a flight from anger. In this case, the symbolic meaning of the fat is a "Fuck you!" [1]

Thus, the eating is serving two functions: it expresses the anger indirectly, and the "stuffing" of food prevents the angry feelings from being expressed overtly.[2]

Richard Stuart, the former psychological director of Weight Watchers and a pioneer in the behavioral treatment of obesity, agrees that eating may be a means of expressing anger. He does not, however, limit the connection between anger and eating to women exclusively: "The fact that overweight children sometimes learn to cram food into their mouths as a means of expressing anger against their parents is an illustration of self-directed anger. Unfortunately, many learn to carry this same frustrated and self defeating response into adulthood."[3]

Although eating is frequently seen as a means of venting suppressed anger, *not* eating may serve the same function. Psychoanalyst Alan Goodsitt described the anger expressed by the anorexic's refusal to eat:

For the most part, anorexics find it difficult or impossible to be angry. Anger is disavowed. Nevertheless, an observer may see it written on the anorexic's face or expressed in her behavior. For example, an anorexic frequently stops eating when her mother or anyone else is pleased by her eating. In the anorexic's profound stubbornness, negativism, and oppositionalism, anger is apparent.[4]

The relationship between suppressed anger and eating (or not eating) is so well accepted by therapists of differing persuasions that many treatment programs for eating disorders address expressing anger.[5] Typically the goal of therapy is to have the patients recognize their anger and learn to express it directly. It is assumed that once the anger is expressed, eating problems will decrease.

How do you know if you have suppressed anger? There is no foolproof method of knowing, but your body and behavior may give you some clues. If you think that you don't have the right to be angry and you feel uneasy in situations in which you are tempted to get angry, it is likely that you are suppressing anger. Trudy's many physical symptoms were probably related to the angry feelings that she was not expressing. Although the relationship between anger and physiological processes is not well understood, if you have been experiencing unexplained physical symptoms—headaches, stomach pain and muscle aches, for example—ask yourself if they might be a sign of suppressed anger. Another clue to look for is frequent complaining about someone to somebody else. When Sandy complains to Melissa about Jennifer but never discusses her complaints directly with Jennifer, she is probably suppressing anger.

In this chapter, I will present methods for separating eating from both overt anger and suppressed anger. Once you understand the types of situations that typically make you angry, it may be possible to deal with them so that anger, either suppressed or expressed, and eating are not necessary.

Sex Differences

Susie Orbach is one of many writers who have suggested that expressing anger directly is especially difficult for women.[6] Women might be seen as unfeminine or "bitchy" if they become overtly angry. In contrast, men are discouraged from expressing any emotions other than anger. It is "unmanly" to be sad or afraid ("big boys don't cry"), but anger is expected following an injustice or slight. In the best-seller, *The Dance of Anger,* Harriet Goldhor Lerner describes two types of unsuccessful strategies that women use to deal with anger. The "nice lady syndrome" is the anger-suppressing attempt to avoid conflict at all costs. The second approach, the "bitchy" woman, is easily angered but is equally ineffective in getting her needs met.[7] Despite the commonsense appeal of these analyses, research suggests that men and women are not so different in expressing anger. Carol Tavris reviewed the research and concluded that they are similar in their tendency to feel angry, although they may not feel angry about the same things.[8] Apparently men have to suppress anger too.[9] Privates are not allowed to be angry with sergeants, workers cannot yell at bosses, and some husbands won't get angry with their wives. Even Vince suppressed some of his anger. Once I had to cancel an appointment with him because of another obligation. At the time he accepted the cancellation without complaint. Several months later he told me how angry he had been with me.

In a recent study, Beverly Kopper found that gender does not determine the ability to express anger effectively. Nevertheless, a comparison of sex role types showed that traditionally feminine individuals reported a greater tendency to control anger than less feminine women.[10] It may be that the prohibitions against the expression of anger affect only women like Trudy who were raised to be traditionally female. The rest of the female population is just as likely to express anger as men are.

Coping with Anger

If some of your emotional eating is tied to anger, overt and obvious like Vince's or suppressed like Trudy's, your goal will be to decrease the need to be angry. Once you understand the types of situations that typically make you angry, you may be able to deal with them so that anger and eating are not necessary. But first you need to deal with the belief that if you don't express anger, your mental and physical health will suffer. Much popular writing has stressed the beneficial effects of expressing anger. In one popular self-help book, unexpressed anger is conceptualized as a "slush fund" building up in the body until it ultimately produces ulcers, high blood pressure, depression, and various other physical and psychological maladies. The author suggests that expressing anger produces a "good, clean feel," "increased self-esteem and the feel of real peace with one's self and others."[11] The implication is that as long as you don't become violent, expressing anger is good for your physical and mental health. The reality is that expression of anger is a mixed blessing. What happens when you express your anger to a child? Even if the child has been thoroughly obnoxious, watching him or her cry is not likely to increase your self-esteem or make you feel at peace with yourself. Similarly the effects of anger on health are not clear-cut. One study relating anger to blood pressure found that other factors— age, race, social class, and the reason for the anger—affected blood pressure. In another study, the relationship between systolic blood pressure and suppressed anger was significant for white men, almost significant for black men, and insignificant for women. Suppressed anger was unrelated to diastolic blood pressure regardless of gender or race.[12] There doesn't seem to be an obvious conclusion from these findings other than that sweeping statements about the benefits of expressing anger are oversimplifications.[13] I tend to agree with Dr. Tavris: "There are different angers, involving different processes and having different consequences to our mental and physical health. No single remedy fits all. Sometimes suppressed hostility can aggravate stress and illness, but sometimes suppressed hostility is the best thing for you. It used to be called common courtesy."[14]

Thinking Angry Thoughts

Recall from chapter 6 that anger is a *belief* that you have been slighted that causes painful feelings and a desire for revenge. Psychologist Raymond Novaco suggests that maintaining a "task orientation" rather than an "ego orientation" toward the provocation will decrease the likelihood of getting angry and increase the likelihood of making effective changes. Instead of getting angry when you have been provoked, use the internal arousal in your body as a signal to do something. Getting angry is usually disruptive and rarely helps you accomplish what you need to do to improve the situation.[15] Frequently getting angry just teaches others not to take you seriously (this is what happens to the "bitchy woman").

I am not suggesting that there are *never* any reasons to get angry. Anger can be logical and useful to motivate you to do something to change the situation. Consider Vince's anger with his boss and his anger with his father. In both instances, he had ample justification for being angry. His boss frequently criticized him for not filling out his order forms accurately when, in reality, Vince made no more mistakes than any of the other salesmen. Many of the comments his boss made to him were tinged with sarcasm, implying that Vince was lazy or incompetent. Being angry with the boss could be useful. The anger, properly channeled, could help motivate Vince to find a new job or increase his commissions in his current job; either would be a desirable outcome. In contrast, Vince's anger with his father was self-defeating. His father had died from an alcohol-related illness. Now, more than ten years later, there was nothing Vince could do to make peace with his father, much less tame his father's violent and emotionally abusive behaviors. Vince recognized that being angry with his father did not help to accomplish anything worthwhile but did lead to bad feelings and increased eating. The same judgment of useful versus self-defeating (or task orientation versus ego orientation) can be made with suppressed anger after you have recognized that you are feeling angry.

Review your Emotional Eating Record to find instances of eating precipitated by anger. Try to recall what made you angry. Was your anger useful? Did it motivate you or help to reach a goal? In all likelihood, if the anger was productive, your energies would be directed toward accomplishing a goal so you would not need to eat. If the anger is self-defeating, you need to work on the thinking that produces the anger. To start, find two instances of angry eating and complete the antecedent-thought-emotion (A-T-E) sequence in the spaces below:

Antecedent: _____   Antecedent: _____

Thought: _____   Thought: _____

Emotion: _____   Emotion: _____

Antecedents

Remember that the antecedent is usually something that happens in your environment—a slight or a provocation like a driver cutting you off in traffic or an insulting comment from one of the neighborhood kids, for example. The antecedent could also be something that somebody does not do. For example, you are sitting in a restaurant and the waiter takes the order from the people at the table next to you even though you arrived first. Occasionally the antecedent may be something that doesn't involve you but an event that you observe offends your sense of fairness or justice—perhaps reading an article about the brutality of Serbs toward Bosnians or watching someone sneak in a parking space that another motorist had been patiently waiting for. In these examples, nothing happens to you and you are not involved, but the incident nonetheless can be an antecedent to anger.

Thoughts

Next, try to identify the thought that followed. This is important because it is not the antecedent itself that causes the anger; it is your thought about it. In the restaurant example, you got angry only after you recognized that the waiter served the other table first, and then you thought that it was unfair. Probably there have been dozens of times you've been in a restaurant and a waiter has served others who came in after you, but you did not notice, did not think it was unfair, and did not get angry. Or perhaps you did notice but also noticed that the waiter had just come on duty so did not know that you were there first. In these instances, the antecedent was the same, but you didn't think it was unfair, so you were not angry. It was the thought of unfairness that caused the anger.

Often the thought responsible for anger is irrational. Several of Dr. Burns's Ten Forms of Twisted Thinking are usually responsible for anger (see pp. 95–97).[16] Many angry feelings can be traced back to implicit *should* statements. We have expectations for how people and things are supposed to behave, and when they don't meet our expectations, we are angry. Your daughter *should* have sent a thank-you note for the gift, the jeans *should* not shrink after being washed, the waiter *should* know that you got there first. Vince often expressed the idea that his boss *should* have appreciated his salesmanship. In a perfect world, people do just what you would like them to do, and jeans never shrink. This is not terribly realistic, though. Not everyone would agree with your list of *should* statements, and you might not agree with my list. Some people don't care about thank-you notes, and others purposely buy their jeans too big so that they can shrink them for a tight fit.

Given that we live in a less than perfect world, populated by thoroughly fallible fellow human beings, it is more rational to think in terms of preferences or wishes rather than absolute *should* statements. If your wishes are unfulfilled, you will be confused, disappointed, or inconvenienced, but you do not have to get angry. Besides, what good would getting angry do? Would the world be more perfect?

Another type of twisted thinking that frequently leads to anger is a combination of mind reading and blaming. Mind reading is one type of jumping to conclusions without sufficient evidence; blaming occurs when responsibility for something negative is attributed to someone else. Thus Trudy was mind reading when she assumed that her physician's refusal to show her the medical report was motivated by his need to "play a power trip." As a result of the conflict with her mother, Trudy was sensitive to any attempt to control her. She assumed, without sufficient evidence, that this is what the doctor was trying to do. She then blamed him for her frustration at not knowing what was in the report. Once Trudy recognized that she was mind reading and blaming, she considered alternative explanations for her doctor's behavior. As she discussed these possibilities, I could see her becoming less angry. If she had done the same analysis the day before, she would not have had to binge.

A third common illogical type of thought that can cause anger is labeling. Vince frequently described his boss as a "pushy little jerk." It is true that Vince's boss was 5 feet, 4 inches, so conceivably he could be considered little, but *pushy* and *jerk* are not so easily defined. In all likelihood, the boss was under some pressure to meet his sales quotas. Being "pushy" was his none-too-effective way of motivating Vince to do better. Many of the "jerk" behaviors probably were the result of the boss's being intimidated by Vince's size and his temper. The boss's uneasiness with Vince would make it difficult to communicate without some awkwardness. Labeling cannot be defended on rational grounds. It serves to justify and sometimes to increase angry feelings. Calling his boss a "pushy little jerk" allowed Vince to harbor resentment and rationalize angry outbursts. It also increased the likelihood that he would eat to feel stronger.

Perhaps you are uncomfortable with the idea of challenging the twisted thinking that causes anger. If you put yourself in Vince's shoes, you would not like his boss's comments, or maybe you feel that the physician was withholding Trudy's report for some personal reason. While it's unlikely that we will ever know their motives, if you determine that your anger is not based on twisted thinking, then you can decide to do something to correct the situation. Checking your thoughts to make sure that they are rational will not prevent you from taking a corrective action. Once Vince recognized that the boss was supervising in the only way he knew how, Vince stopped calling him a jerk and made several attempts to discuss their differences. When Vince was convinced that the boss would not change, he started looking for another job.

Go back to the two instances of anger you identified above. In the spaces below, write in the thought(s), the type of twisted thinking implicit in the thought, and a rational response to the thought.

Date _____ Time _____ Antecedent _____

Thought	Type of Twisted Thinking	Rational Response
_____	_____	_____
_____	_____	_____
_____	_____	_____
_____	_____	_____

Date _____ Time _____ Antecedent _____

Thought	Type of Twisted Thinking	Rational Response
_____	_____	_____
_____	_____	_____
_____	_____	_____
_____	_____	_____

As you identified the twisted thinking and thought of the rational response, did you find that the intensity of your anger decreased?

Using Your Angry Feelings

If you have examined the thoughts that are producing your anger and decide that they are rational, you can use the anger to motivate yourself to make changes. If you are confident that your anger is rational and you know that you have expressed it appropriately, it is less likely that you will need to eat. Robert Alberti and Michael Emmons, pioneers in the study of assertive behavior, offered suggestions for the assertive expression of anger: "Be spontaneous; don't wait and let it build up resentment; state it directly, avoid sarcasm and innuendo; use honest, expressive language; avoid name-calling, put-downs, and physical attacks."[17] They suggest that instead of accusations or name calling, you use phrases like, "I am very angry," "I think that's unfair," or "I get mad when you say [do] that" and then describe the problem and suggest a solution. Recognize that this process may have to be repeated, and there is no guarantee of success. Trudy assertively expressed her objections to her mother's interference many times before giving up. Although she was unsuccessful in changing her mother's behavior, Trudy reduced her emotional eating by recognizing that she was angry, deciding the anger was rational, and expressing it assertively.

Anger, overt or suppressed, can give rise to emotional eating. Use your Emotional Eating Record to find the antecedents and identify the thoughts that follow. Evaluate the rationality of the thoughts by referring to the ten forms of twisted thinking. If the anger-inducing thoughts are irrational, challenge them. If they are rational, assertively communicate your anger.

Sex, Marriage, and Weight

Perhaps the surgeon general should issue a warning to all engaged couples: CAUTION: MARRIAGE MAY BE HAZARDOUS TO YOUR WEIGHT. One survey of nine thousand women responding to a questionnaire in a national magazine found that on the average, women who had been unhappily married for 13 years gained 42.6 pounds. Even happily married women gained an average of 18.4 pounds in thirteen years of marriage. Men were not immune to the fat-producing effects of matrimony. Happily married husbands gained an average of 19 pounds, while their less happy peers gained 38 pounds.[1] Since weight typically increases with age and the survey might not be representative of the population at large, we need to be cautious in drawing conclusions. Nevertheless, it appears that marriage is associated with gaining weight, and being unhappily married makes it worse.

Why does marriage produce weight gain? Although the survey didn't answer this question, it is likely that life-style changes account for some of the gains. Perhaps men who had been physically active when younger now play golf every other weekend instead of playing basketball every day. Or a young woman who shares an apartment with a friend gets married and finds herself preparing full meals for her family rather than grabbing a bite to eat.

Especially for women who don't work outside the home, marriage produces an environment that makes weight gain likely. Richard Stuart and Barbara Jacobson describe the job of housewife (or homemaker or full-time mother) as "the most fattening job in the world."[2] The worker is given continuous, easy access to food all day long. Many of her responsibilities—shopping, cooking, and clean-up—require contact with food. Some of her other tasks are sufficiently boring to make eating a welcome break from the monotony. Even when no food is within reach, the successful housewife is likely to be thinking about food. She is supposed to be planning meals, finding new recipes, and clipping coupons for foods on sale at the supermarket. Working in a socially isolated environment (the home), there is less need for her to be concerned about maintaining her appearance and a greater likelihood that she will be lonely.

More than the change in routine following marriage can produce weight gain; the emotions induced by being married can affect eating too. In this chapter I will describe three common patterns of emotional eating that are related to sexual and marital issues. After reading about these patterns, check your Emotional Eating Records to see if some of your eating may be related to these themes. Pay particular attention to the entries with a question mark or blank space in the Emotion column. Also, check the Location/People column for clues.

Fat as a Chastity Belt

Phyllis, a thirty-eight year-old wife, mother, and college student, is an example of the "chastity belt" pattern. Phyllis was adopted by a minister and his wife. Within a year of the adoption, her mother became pregnant. Lisa, Phyllis's new sister, quickly became the center of attention. Throughout her child-hood, Phyllis tried several strategies to earn her parents' affec-tion but always seemed to come in second behind Lisa. As a child, her clowning behavior sometimes got her in trouble in school, but her good grades prevented teachers from becom-ing too angry with her. Her mother was not as understanding. She was frequently embarrassed by Phyllis's failure to behave like a proper minister's daughter. As an adolescent, Phyllis was rebellious but managed to avoid major problems with drugs or legal troubles. When she was seventeen, she had a series of sexual involvements that were ended when she got pregnant and married Dan. Within three years, Dan aban-doned her and their daughter, leaving Phyllis dependent on her parents again. After divorcing Dan, she met Chet, whom she married after a brief courtship.

Phyllis had been married to Chet for eleven years when she first came to see me. She had mixed feelings about their mar-riage. Although she had never felt too attracted to him, she admired Chet's stability. He worked at two jobs to support their family. Unlike her first husband, Chet showed no incli-nation to go out drinking with his buddies, flirt with other women, or spend his weekends hunting or fishing. He spent most of his free time at home, on the sofa, watching television until he fell asleep.

She appreciated Chet's dependability, but found him unat-tractive and boring, and she missed the sexual excitement she had had with her first husband. Phyllis complained that with Chet, the frequency of their lovemaking had declined to less than once a month. She was especially frustrated because Chet seemed perfectly content. She felt guilty because Chet's finan-cial support enabled her to go back to college, yet she couldn't help fantasizing about having an affair with one of her pro-fessors. Phyllis told me that as long as she was overweight, no one would be attracted to her. In addition, as long as she was fat, she wouldn't be comfortable taking her clothes off. On the other hand, if she did lose weight, "Chet might not be good enough for me." The 60 pounds Phyllis had gained during her eleven years of marriage served as a self-imposed chastity belt. It ensured that she would not find herself in a situation that would jeopardize her marriage. Unfortunately, it left her feeling lonely, sexually frustrated, and mildly depressed.

Although Phyllis was aware of the protection her fat afforded her, she was not consciously intending to gain weight. For many years, she had used food to compensate for her feelings of boredom and loneliness. She appreciated Chet's devotion but felt lonely because they rarely did things together and didn't communicate well. With time, her dissatisfaction and her weight increased. Her emotional eating served two purposes: it helped her cope with the loneliness at the time, and over the long term, it prevented her from having an affair.

Apparently this pattern is common. Stuart and Jacobson report that a "substantial number" of the women responding to their survey believed that temptation to have an affair increases when they lose weight. Several studies have demonstrated an increase in sexual interest after major weight losses. Following intestinal bypass operations and substantial weight loss, the majority of formerly obese women surveyed reported an increase in sexual interest and activity.[3] Two studies suggest that husbands became anxious and jealous following their wives' weight losses.[4] These studies were limited to very obese women who underwent a drastic surgical procedure to reduce.

Sam Catalano, a graduate student working with me, wanted to see if the effects of weight loss were as significant for less obese women who lost weight by more conventional methods. He placed advertisements in several newspapers to recruit people who had recently tried to lose weight. Respondents who were within 10 pounds of their goal were classified as successful dieters, those who had 10 to 20 pounds were intermediate, and those with more than 20 pounds to lose were unsuccessful dieters. For both men and women, participants closest to their target weights reported the greatest frequency of sexual behavior. A questionnaire intended to assess motivations for sex indicated that recognition and competition were important reasons for successful dieters to have sex. It appeared that once they had lost weight, sex was one way successful dieters asserted themselves. Being sexual demonstrated that they were "as good as everybody else."[5] This was exactly how Phyllis felt: if she lost weight, she would be good enough so that she would not have to settle for a secure but boring relationship.

Fat as Armor

Phyllis used her excess weight to keep her from acting on her sexual desires. A closely related pattern occurs when a woman lacks confidence in her own ability to cope with advances from sexually aggressive men. Rather than dealing with this frightening situation, she gains weight to prevent sexual demands. Diane, twenty-eight years old, illustrates this pattern.

Diane had it all: an Ivy League education, a loving husband, a management job with a rapidly growing company, and a new BMW. She also had 40 extra pounds. When she married Carl eight years earlier, she weighed 125. Her weight had been steadily increasing since then.

Diane described several incidents in which she was the recipient of unwanted sexual attention. As a high school senior, the conductor of the school orchestra would drive her to rehearsals. She felt very awkward when he told her how much he liked her and that someday they would get married. In college, her piano instructor tried to kiss and fondle her. Diane was quite pretty and when she was thin, her friendliness was incorrectly interpreted as sexual availability. Diane understood the relationship of sex to weight. She told me, "When

I'm thin, I'm more attractive to men. It makes me uncomfortable. Since I've been heavy, I haven't been a sex object."

Diane understood the connection between weight and sex, so you might think it would be easier for her to learn to say no to men instead of gaining weight to keep them away, but Diane had difficulty asserting herself. As a child, she was taught to avoid conflict no matter what the cost. Her parents never fought with each other when the children were present. When there was a disagreement, her mother would not speak to her father for several days and made him sleep on the sofa, but they did not argue. Diane was taught not to "talk back" to adults.

Diane came to see me not because of her weight but because she was dreading a trip back East to visit her parents. Despite her many accomplishments, her parents were preoccupied with her appearance, especially her weight. We worked on her self-esteem and developing assertive responses that she could use when her parents made inappropriate comments about how she looked (e.g., "Diane, you're becoming a little porker these days"). With some practice, she learned to communicate assertively with her parents, and the visit went well. Her success with her parents increased her self-confidence; she was more comfortable expressing her opinion at work, and disagreeing with her husband, and she started losing weight. Several months later, she wrote me a letter stating that she had made additional progress and "didn't feel at war with food anymore."

Diane's use of fat to protect herself from unwanted sexual advances is common. In a study of patients undergoing psychoanalysis, 47.7 percent of the obese patients indicated that they used eating to avoid sexual relationships.[6] Although patients in analysis may not be representative of all obese individuals, this finding suggests that Diane is hardly unique. Several hundred of Stuart and Jacobson's respondents "had disappointing or frightening sexual experiences they attributed to their weight loss, and many were determined to prevent these from ever happening again."[7]

Why do some women use weight gain to avoid sex? Virtually all cultures use some body characteristics as the basis for judging sex appeal.[8] For example, in the Karagwe kingdoms of East Africa, the most alluring sexual partners were found in the king's harem. All were massively obese.[9] Americans see obesity quite differently; we view obesity as being a sexual "turn-off." Researcher Marcia Millman suggested that "for women, the association of obesity with asexuality largely stems from the assumption that fat women have chosen not to make their bodies attractive, chosen to be unfeminine, to avoid sexuality and sexual relations."[10]

Many women, especially if they have been fat throughout their adolescence and early adult years, may never have learned how to handle the attention and suggestive comments from men. Some women, like Diane, have had frightening experiences and lack confidence in their ability to cope with future repetitions. Under these circumstances, it is not surprising that they would use fat as protective armor.

With the chastity belt and armor patterns, eating and weight gain are linked specifically to sex. In marriage, eating and weight gain can also have a major impact on virtually all other aspects of the relationship.

Fat to Maintain Equilibrium

Family therapists view marriage as a complex system governed by well-defined rules in which each partner gives something and receives something else in return. Although these rules may not be stated, both partners clearly understand them. For example, in many families, it is assumed that the wife will take care of the house, while the husband is responsible for main-

taining the yard and cars. According to family system theorists, ongoing interactions take place within the family to
preserve this homeostasis. An analogy is made to a thermostat: when it gets cold, the thermostat turns the furnace on to
bring the temperature in a house back to a comfortable level.
In a family, anything that threatens to disrupt the established
balance will trigger a response intended to restore the equilibrium.[11]

When one marital partner, typically a wife, has been fat for
some time, her feelings of unattractiveness, her frequent dieting or failure to diet, and her concern about weight fluctuations all become part of the homeostatic balance in the
relationship. Starting to lose weight threatens the balance and
is likely to elicit behaviors from the spouse that attempt to
restore the balance typically by undermining weight loss. In a
study of fourteen couples, Richard Stuart showed some of the
ways this happens. He made tape recordings of dinnertime
conversations between husbands and their wives who were
clients in a weight-reduction program. He found that husbands brought up food as a topic of conversation seven times
as often as wives, husbands offered food to their wives four
times as often as wives did to the husbands, and for each instance of praise for the wives' eating behavior, there were
twelve criticisms of it. Although it is risky to generalize from
these data because they were derived from a limited sample, it
seems that these fourteen husbands were undermining their
wives' weight-loss efforts. Unhelpful comments during dinner
are not the only methods husbands can use to keep their wives
fat. Some common tactics Stuart and Jacobson found include:

- Pressure, demands, or nagging that she lose weight.
- Comparing her body or weight with other women.
- Making negative comments about other overweight
  women.

- Complaining about costs of health clubs, diet foods, or other weight-loss efforts.
- Demanding that she prepare fattening meals.
- Insisting on having snacks nearby.
- Offering to go shopping but buying the wrong foods.
- Complaining when she leaves to go to exercise or group meetings.[12]

In another study Dr. Stuart interviewed fifty-five husbands of overweight women. While virtually all of them said they would like their wife to lose weight, twenty-one said they were afraid that there would be a divorce if they did lose, seventeen expressed fear that their wife would be unfaithful (the chastity belt pattern), and twenty-seven were afraid that they would lose their "bargaining position in arguments."[13] This last response helps explain how weight loss upsets the equilibrium in a relationship. It's likely that when an overweight wife has a complaint about her husband or there is an argument or even a disagreement, all he has to do is to make reference to her weight. If she objects to his drinking or thinks that he should do chores instead of watching football, he can respond that she has neglected to follow her diet. If she pressures him to take an exam for a promotion at work, he agrees to do so—as soon as she loses weight. Since being fat is visible "proof" of her weakness, laziness, or lack of virtue, she has lost her credibility in the dispute, he does not need to change, and the equilibrium is maintained.

Divorcing Fat from Sex and Marriage

If you recognize any of these patterns in your own behavior, the basic strategy for change is to separate eating from sexual and marital issues. Especially if the pattern is well established, change may be difficult and can elicit negative responses from others; nevertheless, understanding the possible obstacles to change will enable you to develop effective strategies for overcoming them. For both the chastity belt and armor patterns, we will use the same basic approach: overcoming the anxieties behind these patterns. To change the equilibrium in a marriage will require a different strategy. You will need to teach others that you have the sole responsibility for your weight.

Unlocking the Chastity Belt

Everyone, regardless of weight, has sexual feelings and must make choices about sexual behavior. If you have been using weight as a chastity belt, you have been protecting yourself from the anxiety that frequently accompanies sexual decisions. When you succeed in separating the issue of your weight from your sexuality, you may have to confront this anxiety. We can use the A-T-E format to do this.

For Phyllis, the prospect of weight loss was frightening. As we explored these issues, it became apparent that she was making several assumptions about herself that were not entirely rational. Using the A-T-E format, we examined the thoughts that caused the fear:

Antecedent: _Weight loss_ _____

Thought(s): _1. I'll have an affair with my professor._ ____

2. I won't be ashamed of my body so I'll become

a "nympho." _____

3. Chet won't be good enough for me. We'll get

divorced. _____

Emotion: _Anxiety_ _____

There are several examples of twisted thinking here. Her first thought is an example of fortune telling. Although she did have brief sexual relationships when she was a single teenager, her current circumstances are quite different. Since she still has bad feelings about her earlier sexual behavior and takes her marriage vows seriously, it is irrational to predict that she will not be able to control her sexual impulses even if she is attracted to her professor. The second thought is equally irrational. When Phyllis loses weight, it is quite likely that she will be more comfortable with her body, but her assertion that she will lose all sense of modesty is all-or-nothing thinking. It is equally irrational for her to use the term *nympho* to describe herself. This is labeling. Even if she had several affairs, the label *nympho* focuses on only one aspect of her behavior. The third thought is fortune telling. There isn't enough evidence to predict that Phyllis will divorce Chet. In fact, once she starts to lose weight Chet might be persuaded to participate in aerobics with her and lose weight himself. Aside from making him more attractive, the joint activity could make their time together more interesting. Even if Chet refused to participate, Phyllis could tell him about her dissatisfactions, and if necessary they could go to marriage counseling before she gave up on the marriage.

Although a discussion of all the different sources of sexual anxiety is beyond the scope of this book, most can be overcome by examining the thoughts implicit in the fears.[14] It is far better to confront the source of the anxiety than to continue to use fat as a means of avoiding sex.

Giving Up Armor

If you have been using fat as a way of avoiding unwanted sexual attention, changing eating habits and losing weight will produce uneasy, anxious feelings. As was the case with the chastity belt pattern, to the extent that you decrease your reliance on fat as armor, you depend on your own ability to control your sexual behavior. If you're afraid that you won't be able to do this, you will become anxious.

Diane and I discussed what would happen if she lost weight. We used the A-T-E format to identify the thoughts that were responsible for her anxiety. The following sequence emerged:

Antecedent: *Weight loss*

Thought(s): *1. I won't be able to handle unwanted sexual attention.*

2. Carl will be jealous and divorce me.

Emotion: *Anxiety*

We discussed the rationality of both thoughts. Although she is making predictions about the future, the first thought is not entirely irrational (fortune telling) because she does have some evidence to support part of the prediction. In the past, when she was thinner she did get unwanted attention, and although she is older and in a new environment, it is possible that this would happen again. The other part of the prediction—that she would not be able to handle the attention—is a combination of overgeneralization ("Since I had difficulty dealing with my piano instructor, I will have difficulty dealing with all sexually aggressive men") and fortune telling. As a child, Diane was taught not to disagree or refuse requests, but Diane isn't a child anymore. She is a mature, competent adult. There is no reason to believe that she is incapable of learning to resist sexual advances. After we came up with responses, some humorous and some unequivocally firm, she had more confidence in her ability to cope. Although she still did not like the idea of being propositioned, it became much less threatening for her.

If you can identify either the chastity belt or armor (or both) pattern in yourself, fill in the spaces below:

Antecedent: _____

Thought(s): 1._____

_____

2._____

_____

3._____

_____

Emotion: *Anxiety* _____

Now for each of the thoughts, identify the type of twisted thinking, using the list on pages 95–97, and write in a more rational response. Remember that the rational response should not be a "pie-in-the-sky" or "power-of-positive-thinking" dream. Diane had to learn what to say in response to unwanted attention. Phyllis planned on involving Chet in her exercise, and if that didn't work, she was prepared to try marriage counseling to solve their problems. Try to make your rational response equally specific. They could include learning new behaviors or seeking professional help.

Thought	Type of Twisted Thinking	Rational Response

Do not expect quick or dramatic changes. You will find that as your thinking changes and you gain confidence in your new abilities to handle sexual challenges, the need for the safety these patterns provide will decrease.

Establishing a New Equilibrium

Regardless of what other people may say or do, recognize that only you control your eating. When you accept this principle, your eating and weight will be removed from the homeostatic balance of the relationship. Unfortunately, not everyone accepts this idea; perhaps you don't either. If you have gotten used to comments and suggestions from others, you may have forgotten that you are still the only one who can determine what you eat.

Over the long term, no one can make you eat or make you not eat. This truth has been demonstrated to me many times by women with eating disorders. Michele, a twenty-four-year-old bulimic client, told me about her stay in an impatient hospital treatment unit. In order to prevent her binges and purges, she was kept on the unit, not allowed to have any food in her room, had to eat with a group, and for two hours after each meal, she was followed whenever she went into the bathroom. Despite the staff's best efforts to control her eating, Michele managed to binge and purge anyway. Marie, an anorexic college student told me that when she was in a hospital unit, she was fed intravenously and then spent hours doing aerobics to burn up calories. Pat, a middle-aged librarian married to a teacher, described her husband's attempt to prevent her from eating ice cream. He would forbid her to buy ice cream, throw it away if he found any in the freezer, and shame her if he found out she had stopped for ice cream. Do you think his efforts decreased her ice cream consumption?

No one could make Michele, Marie, or Pat eat or not eat—and no one can make you eat or not eat. The choice is yours. Unless there is a famine, if someone tries to prevent you from eating, I'm sure you'll be able to find a way to outsmart them. When you, your spouse, your family, and anyone else you know accepts this truth, it will become possible to separate your eating from the unresolved issues in your relationships. Therefore, the first step in changing is to let other people know that although you appreciate their concern for you, making decisions about food is something that only you can do. You may find that it is difficult for others to relinquish their role as guardian of your food intake, but with your persistent training, they will learn.

You do not need to feel ashamed if someone "catches" you eating food. It is your choice to make, and even if you agree that it was a bad choice and feel guilty, you do not owe anyone else an explanation or an apology. When someone comments about your eating, the best response is not to get angry. Don't become exasperated and give up either. Instead, memorize a simple phrase that summarizes your intent to make your own decisions about your food intake. You might say, "I appreciate your concern, but if I'm going to succeed, I need to make

my own decisions about what I eat" or, "Yes, I know that
_____ isn't on my diet, but that was the choice I made." If
you are pressed for an explanation, remember that you don't
owe anyone a justification. You can politely repeat your standard response. If this doesn't satisfy your inquisitor, it is perfectly acceptable to turn the question around and ask, "Why is
it so important to you to keep track of what I eat?" You are
not being rude; you are letting the person know that you refuse
to surrender control of your eating to anyone else. Pause for a
moment and think of responses you could make to your
spouse or anyone else who makes frequent comments about
your eating. Write your responses in the spaces below.

1. _____

_____

2. _____

_____

When you recognize that your choice of food is your responsibility exclusively and insist that others learn that their
comments are inappropriate, you are removing your eating
and weight from the dynamics of the family. Doing this may
present new challenges. Your spouse will need to deal with
disagreements in a straightforward way. This may have the
effect of temporarily increasing the intensity of conflict, but
over the long term it presents the opportunity to resolve issues
that have separated you, to become closer, and to establish a
new equilibrium that is not based on your eating or weight.

12

The Decision to Diet

It's time to decide whether to diet. To make an informed decision, let's review your success controlling emotional eating, and then look at some of the other factors that contribute to successful weight loss.

If you have been completing the exercises, you should have a good idea of the types of emotions that make you want to eat. Most emotional eaters recognize instances of eating in response to almost any type of emotional arousal but find that there is a more consistent pattern of eating following one or two emotions. Work on changing these patterns first before going after the more isolated instances of emotional eating. You will decrease your emotional eating by using the A-T-E format to change the thoughts that produce the emotion and then add some of the behavioral methods.

Although the research indicates that depression, anxiety, boredom, loneliness, and anger are the most common causes of emotional eating, you may have found that some of your emotional eating is triggered by a different emotion.[1] You can use many of the methods presented for other types of emotional eating. For example, I don't know of any research linking jealousy with eating. Still, if you find that you eat whenever you feel jealous, you could do an antecedent-thought-emotion analysis on your jealous thinking and substitute more rational thoughts.

Knowing When to Diet

Psychologist Kelly Brownell, who has published some of the most influential recent research on obesity and weight loss, suggests that before starting a diet, it is important to determine your readiness. In other words, given your state of mind, life circumstances, and motivation, is this a good time to start?[2] Let's look at several of the variables that determine readiness to diet, starting with emotional eating.

Emotional Eating

It is not essential to curtail emotional eating completely before starting a weight-reduction program. The idea that complete abstinence is essential comes from twelve-step programs. Although it is obvious what constitutes abstinence from alcohol, the idea of abstinence is not clearly defined when it comes to food. Obviously, you can't completely abstain from eating, or you'd die before too long. So what is abstinence? According to one Overeaters Anonymous member, "abstinence wasn't starving or fasting. It was living without abusing food. It was responding to life directly instead of avoiding it with a few well-timed M&Ms."[3] It is not clear if abstinence meant that this OA member never ate another M&M, ate only a few M&Ms, or ate M&Ms only when she wasn't avoiding life. There is no clear definition of when eating becomes "abuse." I have never seen an unambiguous definition of overeating abstinence; it is not a useful concept when applied to eating. Instead of aiming for a vaguely defined goal like abstinence, it is more realistic to expect, that with continued effort, your emotional eating will decrease. Rather than being angry with yourself for failing to be abstinent, recognize that any behavior change takes time, and some days will be more difficult than others.

The first question that needs to be answered in deciding to diet is, Have you made sufficient progress in controlling emotional eating? If you are not sure, take the Mood Eating Scale (pp. 16–17) again and use the Emotional Eating Record for another week. Compare your score and the amount of emotional eating now with what they were when you got started. Have you made significant changes for the better? Does it look as if you will continue to make progress? If the answer to either question is no, identify the difficulties, go back to the relevant chapters, and continue to work on these patterns before starting a diet. If you can answer yes to both questions, give yourself a pat on the back. You have cleared one of the major stumbling blocks to weight loss. Even if you should decide that you do not want to diet, you still can feel pleased with your accomplishment.

In chapter 4 I briefly discussed the psychological and biological consequences of dieting. Remember that dieting tends to make you more emotional, which could increase your emotional eating. If you have been successfully using the methods presented in this book to control emotional eating, you should be well equipped to deal with any emotions brought on by dieting.

Goals and Attitudes

Your reasons for wanting to lose weight and your expectations regarding how much and how fast you will be able to lose play a role in determining the likelihood of your success. In the spaces that follow, write in your reason or reasons for wanting to lose weight.

1. _____

2. _____

3. _____

In one study, participants at a commercial weight-loss program were asked about their motivations before they began treatment. Those who had internal, enduring reasons like improving their self-esteem or decreasing their health risks were more likely to stick with the program long enough to reach their goals than participants who were motivated by external and temporary reasons.[4] Now review your reasons. Are you dieting to keep someone else happy? Do you want to look good for a class reunion in a few months, or do you just want to buy some new, smaller clothes? Are you trying to prove to someone that you are capable of losing weight? These external or temporary motivations make it less likely that you will follow through on weight-loss plans. It might make sense to postpone dieting until you have more internal reasons.

The next issue to consider is timing. What is the rest of your life like now? If you think back, some years were characterized by changes and turmoil. You went away to college, got married, a parent died, you had a baby, you moved to a new city, had major upheavals at work, got sick, divorced, or retired. Other years, despite the routine stresses, did not present any major new adjustments. Weight loss requires almost constant attention and dedication. The chances are that if you are in the midst of major life changes, you will not be able to devote the time and concentration required to reduce. On the other hand, if your life is relatively settled, you will be better able to focus on a weight-loss plan.

If you do decide to reduce, how much do you expect to lose, and by when? Dr. Brownell suggests that there are two mistaken assumptions implicit in most weight-loss attempts: any body can be molded into an ideal physique and reaching your goal will greatly improve the quality of your life.[5]

With the right combination of diet program, exercise, and perhaps a special potient, can you reach your ideal? Although the idea that we can transform ourselves into anything we would like is an appealing fantasy, it is not true. Your genetic code puts limits on the amount of weight you can lose and determines where the fat on your body will be located. If you have dieted before and reached (or almost reached) your goal, only to see your weight slowly creep back, consider the possibility that your goal may have been too low. Before starting another diet, ask yourself if you can be satisfied with a weight loss that leaves you heavier than your ideal.

Let's examine the second assumption. Granted that weight loss will probably decrease some health risks, is that your only reason for dieting? When you daydream about being thinner, what do you think will be different? Will you do better at work or school? be more successful with the opposite sex? or be happier? Dr. Brownell suggests that many dieters believe that their lives will significantly improve following weight loss, although the evidence suggests that it can be a mixed blessing. If you are single, for example, you may find that you get more attention from the opposite sex but not feel any better about relationships. Chuck, a twenty-two-year-old college student, provides a good example. In a little more than a year, he dropped from 294 to 185 pounds. He bought some new clothes and was quite handsome with his fashionable glasses. Now women were calling Chuck and he had more dates, but he still felt that his relationships were superficial and unsatisfying. Losing weight did not solve his problem of being uncomfortable getting close to women. When you think about being slimmer, are you unrealistically expecting a solution to many of the difficulties in your life? A successful diet will leave you slimmer but with many of the same issues you were wrestling with before.

Setting Goals

Unrealistic weight-loss goals virtually guarantee that you will fail. First, let's consider what your goal weight should be and then how long will it take to reach the goal. If you have a goal in mind, what was the basis for it? If it was a height and weight chart, you may want to reconsider. These charts have only information, not wisdom.

There are several reasons not to base your goal on the "desirable" weight presented in the charts.[6] At best, the desirable weights they specify are averages. They may not be desirable for you. If you have dieted before and you were successful, at least temporarily, try to remember how you felt when you reached your goal weight. Were you able to maintain that weight comfortably, at least for a while? Some dieters are able to be comfortable and only regain after emotional upsets or maintain their losses for months before gradually gaining weight. Other dieters are never comfortable at their goal weight. If you haven't been comfortable at your "desirable" weight, consider a somewhat higher goal weight. You don't need large losses to improve your health risks. According to George Blackburn, a noted obesity researcher, a 5 percent weight loss can cut your risk of having high blood pressure in half.[7]

Forgetting the charts, do you have your own idea of what your weight should be? According to Dr. Brownell, many people have a sense of what weight is realistic for them. By aiming for an unrealistic goal, you could be setting yourself up for failure. The yo-yo pattern of repeated ups and downs is less healthy than maintaining a steady higher weight.[8] If Dr. Brownell is correct, you'd be better off aiming for a realistic loss that you can maintain, even if this results in a goal weight higher than the number on the chart. Can you identify a "realistic weight" that you could reach and maintain? Write this weight in below:

Realistic weight goal:_____ pounds

Keep in mind that for both health and appearance, the real culprit is fat tissue, not pounds. Your weight is only an approximate measure of excess fat. Since muscle tissue is heavier than fat, a muscular person may be too heavy according to the tables but not too fat. The best method for determining the fat content of your body is to be weighed under water. Some fitness centers, hospitals, and university physical education departments have the facilities to do this and report the percentage of fat in your body. Another alternative is caliper measurement of fat at several sites in your body, although the results are not usually as accurate as underwater weighing. For men, ideal body fat should be about 15 to 22 percent of total weight; for women the range is 20 to 27 percent. Once you know how much of your body composition is fat, the person who has weighed you should be able to determine how many pounds you will need to lose in order to bring your body fat into the desirable range. This goal weight is better than a goal taken from a chart.

Even when you have a realistic weight goal, there is some risk in fixating on a single number as the sole criterion for success (or failure). It would be preferable to identify a weight range in which you can feel comfortable. For most people, a weight range could be within 5 to 10 pounds of the weight goal you wrote in. If you have a lot of weight to lose, say, more than 100 pounds, the weight range can be larger. Whatever range you choose, allow yourself to feel comfortable when you are at the higher end of it. Your clothes may still feel snug and you may see yourself as heavier, but this amount of additional weight is not likely to have any adverse health consequences. With the possible exception of your spouse, it is also unlikely that anyone will notice that you are at the higher end of your desired weight range. Just don't allow yourself to go over this limit. Write in a goal weight range below:

My desired weight range: From _____ to _____ pounds

Next, it is important to work out a schedule for meeting your goal. Congressman Ron Wyden, after holding hearings on the diet industry, concluded, "Americans always want a quick fix. It is almost in the chromosomes. We want results in 20 minutes."[9] These fantasies are encouraged by ads promising weight loss if you "give us a week." Yet the truth is that you would not want to lose all your excess weight in a week, even if you could. When weight is lost rapidly, usually water and muscle tissue is lost rather than fat. Although your scale won't know the difference, you will. If you plan on a 1- or 2-pound loss per week, you are more likely to lose fat than muscle. Also, if you accept before you start that there won't be any instant, dramatic changes, it is less likely that you will get discouraged and quit. Before starting a diet, ask yourself if you can be patient and accept a gradual weight loss. If you can be happy only with immediate gratification, it is unlikely that a diet would be successful.

Willingness to Exercise

In chapter 7 I discussed the beneficial effects exercise has on mood and reviewed studies that demonstrate that even mild exercising reduces depression and improves self-concept. It might help to review this material before committing yourself to a new diet.

Although there are very few absolutes when it comes to weight reduction, it is probably true that you should not start another diet unless you are prepared to increase your activity level with a consistent exercise program. As you get older, the number of calories you need to maintain your weight decreases. This means that there is only so much you can lose by cutting consumption before you find yourself at an unhealthy and unrealistically low level of caloric intake. You need to exercise if you are going to lose weight and maintain a healthy diet. Besides the psychological benefits and the calories burned, there is a fringe benefit to exercising. Aerobic exercise increases your metabolism for about twelve hours after you have finished.[10] In other words, if you take a brisk thirty-minute walk, and then come in and watch television, you will burn more calories even when you're just sitting on the sofa.

Before starting a diet, ask yourself if you can make a firm commitment to an exercise program. Review the seven suggestions on page 104 to develop a realistic plan for yourself that you will be able to follow. Complete your exercise plan by filling in the spaces below.

1. Activity_____

2. Days and times (three times per week—*no* "I don't have the time" excuses):

    1. _____

    2. _____

    3. _____

3. Exercise partner (if any) _____

4. Reward for completing exercise _____

How to Diet

If you have made substantial progress in controlling emotional eating, have confidence in your ability to deal with the possible increased urge to eat emotionally when on a diet, have a realistic weight-reduction goal, and have a firm commitment to an exercise program, this may be the time to start a diet. In addition to choosing a diet—preferably a balanced, low-fat one—it is important that you work on eating habits. This will include learning to eat in response to physical-hunger cues rather than environmental cues, such as the smell or sight of food. If you join a commercial weight-loss program, there will be a habit change segment in your lessons. If you decide to diet on your own, there are several books that could help you to change eating behaviors.[11]

Deciding Not to Diet

Psychologists David Garner and Susan Wooley reviewed more than three hundred studies of both dieting and behavioral treatments for obesity. Although they acknowledged that there may be some people who are able to lose weight and maintain the losses without too much difficulty, overall they concluded that both dieting and behavioral treatments for obesity are ineffective.[12] A recent *New York Times* article about commercial-weight loss programs concluded that "there is little scientific support for claims that commercial diets can provide large-scale, long-term weight loss."[13] If your own experience with diets is equally discouraging, you may reasonably conclude that you don't want to diet. Although this idea makes sense to you, nevertheless you may be reluctant to give up dieting because you are concerned about the health risks of remaining overweight. Several of the women I have worked with found it hard to stop dieting even when they knew that they would never reach their goal weight. Although they knew dieting was pointless, they felt it would be wrong not to "do something" about their weight. If you have these concerns, it may help to examine the alternative ways of reducing your health risks and becoming comfortable without dieting.

Minimizing Health Risks

Many of the health risks attributed to obesity may not be a result of being overweight but rather may be associated with lifestyle choices like heavy drinking, smoking, and a diet high in fats and sugar. If this is the case, then changing the associated behaviors may be easier and more likely to promote good health, than trying to lose weight.

Regardless of your current weight and whether you plan on dieting, exercising is healthy. In one study, the obese men who were moderate exercisers had lower mortality associated with such risk factors as elevated cholesterol, hypertension, and smoking.[14] Exercise plays a crucial role in attempting to lose weight and is at least as important in minimizing health risks if you maintain a heavy body weight. Although it is contrary to conventional wisdom, you can exercise for reasons other than weight loss. It is entirely possible that you can be strong and fit even if you are overweight.

If exercise is so beneficial, why do you rarely see an overweight person jogging or bicycling? If you have a history of being overweight and have tried to exercise before, why did you give it up? Thinking about exercise only in terms of weight loss can be discouraging. Instead, once you have decided not to diet, you can change some of your assumptions about exercise. You can find satisfaction in becoming more fit regardless of your weight.

Maybe you're reluctant to start exercising because you're "too lazy." Before you accept this explanation, let's look at exactly what you mean by "too lazy." Jaclyn Packer, a doctoral candidate in psychology, suggested that social factors decrease the motivation of overweight people to exercise. The stigma associated with being fat results in their avoidance of exercise activities that would subject them to ridicule from others. For most overweight people, riding a bike or jogging in public would feel awkward even if no passers-by made any comments. A fitness center or aerobics class would be worse since it would be difficult to keep up with slimmer peers, and there is always the possibility that the instructor would make a negative comment about being fat.[15] If you are significantly overweight, Packer's findings are no surprise. Given the shame and embarrassment that is often associated with being fat, exercise or any other activity that would draw attention to obesity is likely to be avoided. Instead of thinking of yourself as "too lazy," would it be more accurate to attribute your reluctance to exercise to feelings of awkwardness and a thoroughly reasonable desire to avoid being ridiculed?

Try to find an exercise routine that you can do comfortably, without fear of ridicule. If you have an overweight friend who would also like to be more fit, the two of you could walk or ride bicycles. If you don't have a suitable exercise partner, try a stationary bicycle or use an aerobic dance tape by yourself. Just make sure that you don't pressure yourself to do it faster or longer so that you can burn up more calories.

Regulating Food Intake

If you have spent years dieting, you have had a great deal of practice overruling your body's hunger signals. It may take some time to learn to trust your own judgment about when you are hungry and need to eat. According to *Newsweek* some former dieters are joining groups to support each other in eating naturally. Usually the former dieters fear that they will go on a nonstop binge, eating huge quantities of all the high-calorie foods that were off-limits for so long. Many of the participants report that after an initial flurry, the craving for chocolate chip cookies, ice cream, and other favorite foods decreases. Typically, their weight stabilizes at a level that is heavier than their goal when they had been dieting, but some of the women lost weight eating whatever they wanted.[16] In their review article, Dr. Garner and Dr. Wooley found two studies of nondieting treatments similar to these groups. Both studies reported improvements on various psychological measures and no significant weight gains.[17]

You may find the idea of eating whatever you want frightening. Although it is true that no one knows exactly how much you will eat or at what weight you will stabilize, it is safe to conclude that there will be limits. It is even possible that given free access to chocolate chip cookies, you decide that you're not so crazy about them, and allowed to eat as much as you want, your weight drops. Try an experiment: cautiously start to trust your natural hunger feelings and see what happens.

The Choice Is Yours

By now it is likely that you have had some reactions to the discussion of dieting and not dieting. How are you feeling about starting another diet? If you have made substantial progress controlling emotional eating, are committed to exercising, and are motivated to do what it takes to reach a reasonable goal weight, you stand a good chance of success. If this is not a good time, or you need to do more work on emotional eating, or you have come to the reasonable conclusion that you don't have the drive to stick to a sensible diet, give yourself permission to forgo dieting. You can continue working on emotional eating, allow yourself to eat naturally, and feel comfortable decreasing your health risks by exercising. The choice is yours.

Notes

Chapter 1

1. The latest version of the psychiatric diagnostic manual, DSM-IV, (American Psychiatric Association, *Diagnostic and statistical manual of mental disorders,* 4th ed. Washington, D.C.: APA, Forthcoming) will include a category called binge-eating disorder, so obese binge eaters will be defined as abnormal. Nonetheless, several studies using more traditional psychiatric diagnoses have typically concluded that obesity is not associated with mental illness. For example: T. Hallstrom and H. Noppa, Obesity in women in relation to mental illness, social factors, and personality traits, *Journal of Psychosomatic Research* 25 (1981): 75–82; J. Rodin, Obesity: Why the losing battle? in B. B. Wolman (ed.), *Psychological aspects of obesity: A handbook* (New York: Van Nostrand Reinhold, 1982), pp. 30–87; and T. A. Wadden and A. J. Stunkard, Psychopathology and obesity, *Annals of the New York Academy of Sciences* 499 (1987); 55–65.
2. Much of the writing in the twelve-step movement uses the term *disease* very loosely, either failing to define it or defining it in terms that are so broad that it becomes a meaningless concept. For example, one writer refers to addiction as "a disease of isolation," while another states that a disease has "a set of defined symptoms, the etiology of which is beyond the control of the individual." These examples are from, respectively, J. Greeson, *It's not what you're eating, it's what's eating you* (New York: Pocket, 1990), p. 133, and E. Hampshire, *Freedom from food: The secret lives of dieters and compulsive eaters* (New York: Prentice-Hall/Parkside Recovery, 1990), p. 24.
3. W. Kaminer, *I'm dysfunctional, you're dysfunctional: The recovery movement and other self-help fashions* (Reading, MA: Addison-Wesley, 1992), p. 6.

4. H. I. Kaplan and H. S. Kaplan, The psychosomatic concept of obesity, *Journal of nervous and mental disease* 125 (1957): 181–201.
5. S. Schachter, Obesity and eating, *Science* 161 (1968): 751–756.
6. S. Schachter, R. Goldman, and A. Gordon, Effects of fear, food deprivation and obesity on eating, *Journal of Personality and Social Psychology* 10 (1968): 91–97.
7. E. E. Abramson, and R. A. Wunderlich, Anxiety, fear and eating: A test of the psychosomatic concept of obesity, *Journal of Abnormal Psychology* 79 (1972): 317–321.
8. For a scholarly review of this research, see R. M. Ganley, Emotion and eating in obesity: A review of the literature, *International Journal of Eating Disorders* 8 (1989): 343–361.
9. A. J. Stunkard, Introduction and overview, in A. J. Stunkard (ed.), *Obesity* (Philadelphia: W. B. Saunders, 1980), pp. 1–24.
10. There have been attempts to develop systems for categorizing obese people, but none has been widely accepted. For example, see D. B. Allison and S. Heska, Toward an empirically derived typology of obese persons: Derivation in a nonclinical sample, *International Journal of Eating Disorders* 13 (1993): 93–108.
11. W. Bennett and J. Gurin, *The dieter's dilemma: Eating less and weighing more* (New York: Basic Books, 1982); D.M. Garner and S. C. Wooley, Confronting the failure of behavioral and dietary treatments for obesity, *Clinical Psychology Review* 11 (1991): 729–780.
12. R. E. Keesey, A set-point analysis of the regulation of body weight, in Stunkard, *Obesity*, pp. 144–165.
13. Ganley, Emotion and eating.
14. Ibid.

Chapter 2

1. L. J. Jackson and R. C. Hawkins, *Stress related overeating among college students:* Development of a Mood Eating Scale (unpublished manuscript, 1980).
2. C. Tavris, *Anger: The misunderstood emotion* (New York: Simon and Schuster, 1982), p. 96.
3. J. J. Wurtman et al., Carbohydrate craving in obese people: Suppression by treatments affecting serotoninergic transmission, *International Journal of Eating Disorders* 1 (1981): 2–15.
4. A. J. Stunkard, Eating patterns of obese persons, *Psychiatric Quarterly* 33 (1959): 284–292.

5. American Psychiatric Association, *Diagnostic and statistical manual of mental disorders,* 4th ed. (Washington, DC: APA, forthcoming).
6. N. Youngstrom, Scientists probe traits of binge eating, *APA Monitor* (July 1991): 15.
7. C. G. Sinoway, C. D. Raupp, and J. Newman, Binge eating and bulimia: Comparing incidence and characteristics across universities (paper presented at the annual meeting of the American Psychological Association, Los Angeles, 1985).
8. Youngstrom, Scientists probe traits.
9. Although not bulimic, Penny would have met the criteria for binge eating disorder in the new psychiatric diagnostic manual, DSM-IV.
10. V. M. Lingswiler, J. H. Crowther, and M. A. P. Stephens, Emotional and somatic consequences of binge episodes, *Addictive Behaviors* 14 (1989): 509.
11. V. M. Lingswiler, J. H. Crowther, and M. A. P. Stephens, Emotional reactivity and eating in binge eating and obesity, *Journal of Behavioral Medicine* 10 (1987): 287–299.
12. A. J. Stunkard, W. J. Grace, and H. G. Wolff, The night-eating syndrome: A pattern of food intake among certain obese persons, *American Journal of Medicine* 19 (1955): 78–86; A. J. Stunkard, *The pain of obesity* (Palo Alto, CA: Bull Publishing, 1976).
13. T. J. Coates, Successive self-management strategies towards coping with night eating, *Journal of Behavior Therapy and Experimental Psychiatry* 9 (1978): 181–83.

Chapter 3

1. J. J. Wurtman, *Managing your mind and mood through food* (New York: Harper & Row, 1988), p. 19.
2. See ibid., pp. 252–254, for a list of snacks containing fewer than 200 calories that have enough carbohydrate to increase serotonin production in the brain.
3. Ibid., p. 25.
4. K. Krietsch, L. Christensen, and B. White, Prevalence, presenting symptoms, and psychological characteristics of individuals experiencing a diet-related mood-disturbance, *Behavior Therapy* 19 (1988): 593–604.
5. B. Spock, *Baby and child care,* rev. ed. (New York: Hawthorn, 1968).
6. H. Bruch, *Eating disorders: Obesity, anorexia nervosa, and the person within* (New York: Basic Books, 1973), p. 56.

7. B. Lyman, *A psychology of food: More than a matter of taste* (New York: AVI/Van Nostrand Reinhold, 1989).

8. Bruch, *Eating disorders*, p. 76.

9. For example, psychiatrist, Hilde Bruch wrote about "ownership of the body and its control." See Bruch, *Eating disorders,* pp. 102–104.

10. L. L. Birch, et al., Effects of instrumental eating on children's food preferences, *Appetite* 3 (1982): 125–134; L. L. Birch, D. W. Marlin, and J. Rotter, Eating as the "means" activity in a contingency: Effects on young children's food preference, *Child Development* 55 (1984): 431–439.

11. A. Murcott, *The sociology of food and eating; Essays on the sociological significance of food* (Aldershot, England: Gower Publishing, 1983).

12. B. Lyman, The nutritional values and food group characteristics of foods preferred during various emotions, *Journal of Psychology* 112 (1982): 121–127.

13. L. Ruggiero et al., Forbidden food survey: Measure of bulimics' anticipated emotional reactions to specific foods, *Addictive Behaviors* 13 (1988): 267–274.

14. L. A. Goldfarb, Sexual abuse antecedent to anorexia nervosa, bulimia, and compulsive overeating: Three case reports, *International Journal of Eating Disorders* 6 (1987): 675–680; G. Sloan and P. Leichner, Is there a relationship between sexual abuse or incest and eating disorders? *Canadian Journal of Psychiatry* 31 (1986): 656–660; J. Sours, *Starving to death in a sea of objects. The anorexia nervosa syndrome* (Northvale, NJ: Jason Aronson, 1980).

15. D. L. Coovert, B. N. Kinder, and J. K. Thompson, The psychosexual aspects of anorexia nervosa and bulimia nervosa: A review of the literature, *Clinical Psychology Review* 9 (1989): 169–180.

16. S. E. Finn et al., Eating disorders and sexual abuse: Lack of confirmation for a clinical hypothesis, *International Journal of Eating Disorders* 5 (1986): 1051–1060.

17. E. E. Abramson and G. M. Lucido, Childhood sexual experience and bulimia, *Addictive Behaviors* 16 (1991): 529–532.

18. If you think that you may have had a similar type of sexual experience as a child, it could be useful to see a therapist experienced in dealing with these issues. The following self-help books may also be useful: E. Bass and L. Davis, *The courage to heal* (New York: Harper, 1992), and S. Forward and C. Buck, *Betrayal of innocence* (New York: Viking, 1988).

Chapter 4

1. C. Jakobovits et al., Eating habits and nutrient intakes of college women over a thirty-year period, *Journal of the American Dietetic Association* 71 (1977): 405–411.
2. B. P. Noble, Crash is out, moderation is in, and diet companies feel the pinch, *New York Times,* November 24, 1991, p. 5.
3. J. Polivy and C. P. Herman, Diagnosis and treatment of normal eating, *Journal of Consulting and Clinical Psychology* 55 (1987): 635.
4. J. Polivy and C. P. Herman, *Breaking the diet habit: The natural weight alternative* (New York: Basic Books, 1983), pp. 132–134.
5. Ibid.
6. W. Bennett and J. Gurin, *The dieter's dilemma: Eating less and weighing more* (New York: Basic Books, 1982), p. 34.
7. A. J. Stunkard, The dieting depression: Incidence and clinical characteristics of untoward responses to weight reduction regimens, *American Journal of Medicine* 23 (1957): 77–86.
8. A. J. Stunkard and A. J. Rush, Dieting and depression reexamined: A critical review of reports of untoward responses during weight reduction for obesity, *Annals of Internal Medicine* 81 (1974): 526–533.
9. For example: C. B. Taylor, J. M. Ferguson, and J. C. Reading, Gradual weight loss and depression, *Behavior Therapy* 9 (1978): 622–625; R. R. Wing et al., Mood changes in behavioral weight loss programs, *Journal of Psychosomatic Research* 28 (1984): 189–196, and their Mood and weight loss in a behavioral treatment program. *Journal of Consulting and Clinical Psychology* 51 (1983): 153–155. Stunkard and his colleagues feel that some of the studies failing to find depressed mood were flawed because pretreatment mood was compared with post treatment mood rather than assessing mood continuously throughout the study. In their study, they found that even though there were improvements in mood at the end of treatment, over half of the subjects had significant increases in depression at some point during the course of treatment. Also, they suggest that open-ended interview questions would pick up depressive symptoms that would be missed using the paper-and-pencil questionnaires used in much of the research. T. A. Wadden, A. J. Stunkard, and J. W. Smoller, Dieting and depression: A methodological study, *Journal of Consulting and Clinical Psychology* 54 (1986): 869–871. See also their review of dieting and depression: J. W. Smoller, T. A. Wadden, and A. J. Stunkard, Dieting and depression:

A critical review, *Journal of Psychosomatic Research* 31 (1987): 429–440.

10. A. J. Stunkard, *The pain of obesity* (Palo Alto, CA: Bull Publishing, 1976), p. 83.

11. R. E. Keesey, A set-point analysis of the regulation of body weight, in A. J. Stunkard (ed.), *Obesity* (Philadelphia: W.B. Saunders, 1980) pp. 144–165.

12. A. Keys et al., *The biology of human starvation* (Minneapolis: University of Minnesota Press, 1950).

13. E. E. Abramson and R. A. Wunderlich, Anxiety, fear, and eating: A test of the psychosomatic concept of obesity, *Journal of Abnormal Psychology* 79 (1972): 317–321. See also P. Pliner, P. Meyer, and K. Blankstein, Responsiveness to affective stimuli by obese and normal individuals, *Journal of Abnormal Psychology* 83 (1974): 74–80, and S. Schachter and J. Rodin, *Obese humans and rats* (Potomac, MD: Lawrence Erlbaum Associates, 1974).

14. C. P. Herman and J. Polivy, (1980). Restrained eating, in Stunkard, *Obesity*, p. 222.

15. D. E. Schotte, J. Cools, and R. J. McNally, Film-induced negative affect triggers overeating in restrained eaters, *Journal of Abnormal Psychology* 99 (1990): 317–320.

16. J. Wardle and S. Beales, Control and loss of control over eating: An experimental investigation, *Journal of Abnormal Psychology* 97 (1988): 35–40.

17. J. Polivy and C. P. Herman, Clinical depression and weight change: A complex relation, *Journal of Abnormal Psychology* 85 (1976): 338–340.

18. A. J. Ruderman, Dysphoric mood and overeating: A test of restraint theory's disinhibition hypothesis, *Journal of Abnormal Psychology* 94 (1985): 78–85.

19. P. J. Cooper and R. Bowskill, Dysphoric mood and overeating, *British Journal of Clinical Psychology* 25 (1986): 155–156.

20. J. Rodin, *Body traps: The inner world of weight preoccupation* (paper presented at the meeting of the American Psychological Association, New York, 1987).

21. C. M. Grilo, S. Shiffman, and R. R. Wing, Relapse crises and coping among dieters, *Journal of Consulting and Clinical Psychology* 57 (1989): 488–495.

Chapter 5

1. K. Chernin, *The obsession: Reflections on the tyranny of slenderness* (San Francisco: Harper, 1982), p. 25.
2. A. J. Stunkard, The management of obesity, *New York State Journal of Medicine* 58 (1958): 79–87. For other reviews of the outcome of dieting, see: D. M. Garner and S. C. Wooley, Confronting the failure of behavioral and dietary treatments for obesity, *Clinical Psychology Review* 11 (1991): 729–780; A. J. Stunkard and M. McLaren-Hume, The results of treatment for obesity, *Archives of Internal Medicine* 103 (1959): 79–85; S. M. Garn and P. E. Cole, Do the obese remain obese and the lean remain lean? *American Journal of Public Health* 80 (1980): 351–357.
3. S. R. Doell and R. C. Hawkins, Pleasures and pounds: An exploratory study, *Addictive Behaviors* 7 (1982): 65–69.
4. A. K. Lehman and J. Rodin, Styles of self-nurturance and disordered eating, *Journal of Consulting and Clinical Psychology* 57 (1989): 117.
5. J. Polivy and C. P. Herman, *Breaking the diet habit: The natural weight alternative* (New York: Basic Books, 1983), p. 180.
6. Chernin, *The Obsession*, p. 11.
7. S. Dougherty and J. Sanderson, Farewell Judds, hello Wynnona! *People,* July 13, 1992, p. 37.
8. G. Russell, Bulimia nervosa: An ominous variant of anorexia nervosa, *Psychological Medicine* 9 (1979): 429–448.

Chapter 6

1. P. E. Garfinkel and D. M. Garner, *Anorexia nervosa: A multidimensional perspective* (New York: Brunner/Mazel, 1982), pp. 148–149.
2. R. S. Lazarus, *Emotion and adaptation* (New York: Oxford University Press, 1991), pp. 6–7, 19.
3. W. Mischel, *Introduction to personality: A new look,* 4th ed: (New York: Holt, Rinehart and Winston., 1986), p. 256.
4. S. Schachter, The interaction of cognitive and physiological determinants of emotional state, in L. Berkowitz (ed.), *Advances in experimental social psychology* (New York: Academic Press, 1964), 1:49–80.
5. R. M. Ganley, Emotion and eating in obesity: A review of the literature, *International Journal of Eating Disorders* 8 (1989): 358.
6. R. S. Lazurus, p. 122.

7. S. Freud, Mourning and melancholia, in J. Coyne (ed.), *Essential papers on depression* (New York: New York University Press, 1986) (originally published in 1917).

8. A. T. Beck, *Cognitive therapy and the emotional disorders* (New York: New American Library, 1979), p. 59.

9. D. D. Burns, *Feeling good: The new mood therapy* (New York: William Morrow, 1980).

10. W. Stekel, *Conditions of nervous anxiety and their treatment,* trans. Rosalie Gabler (New York: Dodd, Mead, 1923).

11. C. R. Darwin, *The expression of the emotions in man and animals* (London: John Murray, 1872).

12. R. B. Stuart and B. Jacobson, *Weight, sex, and marriage: A delicate balance* (New York: W. W. Norton, 1987).

13. B. F. Skinner, *Science and human behavior* (New York: Free Press, 1965).

14. F. Perls, R. F. Hefferline, and P. Goodman, *Gestalt therapy: Excitement and growth in the human personality* (New York: Julian Press, 1951).

15. J. E. Young, Cognitive therapy and loneliness, in G. Emery, S. D. Hollon and R. C. Bedrosian (eds.) *New directions in cognitive therapy: A casebook* (New York: Guilford, 1981), p. 140.

16. Aristotle, Rhetoric, in R. McKeon (ed.), *The basic works of Aristotle* (New York: Random House, 1941).

17. J. R. Averill, *Anger and aggression: An essay on emotion.* (New York: Springer-Verlag, 1982).

Chapter 7

1. E. McGrath, *Women and depression: State of the art, state of the science* (Paper presented at the meeting of the American Psychological Association, New Orleans, 1989).

2. American Psychiatric Association, *Diagnostic and statistical manual of mental disorders,* 3d ed. rev. (Washington, D.C.: APA, 1987).

3. B. T. Walsh et al., Bulimia and depression, *Psychosomatic Medicine* 47 (1985): 123–131. Much of the research linking bulimia to depression is summarized in H. G. Pope and J. I. Hudson *New hope for binge eaters* (New York: Harper, 1985).

4. For example: M. F. Folstein, A. Wakeling, and V. DeSouza, Analogue scale measurement of the symptoms of patients suffering from anorexia nervosa, in Vigersky, R. (ed.), *Anorexia nervosa* (New York: Raven, 1977), pp. 21–26.

5. R. J. Wurtmann and J. J. Wurtman, Carbohydrate craving, obesity and brain serotonin. *Appetite* 7 (1986): 99–103, and their Carbohydrates and depression, *Scientific American* (January 1989): 68–75.

6. A. T. Beck, *Cognitive therapy and the emotional disorders* (New York: New American Library, 1979).

7. Ibid., p. 129.

8. D. D. Burns, *The feeling good handbook* (New York: Plume, 1990), pp. 8–11.

9. In addition to *The feeling good handbook*, Dr. Burns has also written, *Feeling good: The new mood therapy* (New York: New American Library, 1981).

10. After reviewing seven studies, Masters et al. concluded that cognitive therapy is at least as effective as any tricyclic antidepressant medication, and may be more beneficial for reducing the likelihood of relapse. J. C. Masters et al., *Behavior therapy: Techniques and empirical findings,* (San Diego: Harcourt Brace Jovanovich, 1987), pp. 424–430.

11. E. J. Doyne et al., Running versus weight lifting in the treatment of depression, *Journal of Consulting and Clinical Psychology* 55 (1987): 748–754.

12. D. J. Ossip-Klein et al., *Journal of Consulting and Clinical Psychology* 57 (1989): 158–161.

13. L. Christensen and R. Burrows, *Dietary treatment of depression* (paper presented at the meeting of the American Psychological Association, New Orleans, 1989).

Chapter 8

1. H. I. Kaplan and H. S. Kaplan, The psychosomatic concept of obesity, *Journal of Nervous and Mental Disease* 125 (1957): 181–201.

2. E. E. Abramson and R. A. Wunderlich, Anxiety, fear and eating: A test of the psychosomatic concept of obesity, *Journal of Abnormal Psychology* 79 (1972): 317–322; S. Schachter, R. Goldman, and A. Gordon, Effects of fear, food deprivation, and obesity on eating, *Journal of Personality and Social Psychology* 10 (1968): 91–97.

3. J. Slochower, Emotional labeling and overeating in obese and normal-weight individuals, *Psychosomatic Medicine* 38 (1976): 131–139.

4. J. Slochower and S. P. Kaplan, Anxiety, perceived control, and eating in obese and normal weight persons, *Appetite* 1 (1980): 75–83.

5. K. Hecht, Oh, come on fatties! *Newsweek,* September 3, 1990, p. 8.

6. D. H. Barlow and J. A. Cerny, *Psychological treatment of panic* (New York: Guilford, 1988), p. 151.
7. This technique was developed by Dr. Victor Frankl, an existential psychiatrist, but is most widely used by behavior therapists. For a more complete description, see V. Frankl, Paradoxical intention: A logotherapeutic technique, *American Journal of Psychotherapy* 14 (1960): 520, and J. Wolpe, *The practice of behavior therapy*, 4th ed. (New York: Pergamon, 1990).
8. G. A. Clum, *Coping with panic: A drug-free approach to dealing with anxiety attacks* (Pacific Grove, CA.: Brooks/Cole, 1990).
9. D. D. Burns, *The feeling good handbook* (New York: Plume, 1990).
10. For a review of the effects of relaxation exercises, see J. Wolpe, *The practice of behavior therapy*, 4th ed. (New York: Pergamon, 1990).
11. These relaxation instructions were taken from K. E. Rudestam, *Methods of self-change: An ABC primer* (Monterey, CA: Brooks/Cole, 1980), p. 23.

Chapter 9

1. G. R. Leon and K. Chamberlain, Emotional arousal, eating patterns, and body image as differential factors associated with varying success in maintaining a weight loss, *Journal of Consulting and Clinical Psychology* 40 (1973): 474–480.
2. E. E. Abramson and S. G. Stinson, Boredom and eating in obese and non-obese individuals, *Addictive Behaviors*. 2 (1977): 181–185.
3. K. Chernin, *The obsession: Reflections on the tyranny of slenderness* (San Francisco: Harper, 1982), p. 11.
4. R. L. Evans and C. M. Dingus, Serving the vulnerable: Models for treatment of loneliness, in M. Hojat and R. Crandall, (eds.), *Loneliness: Theory, research and applications*. (Newbury Park, CA: Sage, 1989).
5. J. F. Schumaker et al., Experience of loneliness by obese individuals, *Psychological Reports* 57 (1985): 1147–1154.
6. R. S. Weiss, Reflections on the present state of loneliness research, in Hojat and Crandall, *Loneliness*, p. 6.
7. J. E. Young, Cognitive therapy and loneliness, in G. Emery, S. D. Hollon, and R. C. Bedrosian, (eds.), *New directions in cognitive therapy* (New York: Guilford Press, 1981).
8. For example, see chapter 10 in P. G. Zimbardo, *Shyness: What it is, what to do about it*, (Reading, MA: Addison-Wesley, 1971).

Chapter 10

1. S. Orbach, *Fat is a feminist issue: The anti-diet guide to permanent weight loss* (New York: Paddington, 1978), pp. 56–57.
2. S. Orbach, *Fat is a feminist issue II: A program to conquer compulsive eating* (New York: Berkeley, 1982).
3. R. B. Stuart, *Act thin, stay thin* (New York: W. W. Norton, 1978), pp. 124–125.
4. A. Goodsitt, Self-psychology and the treatment of anorexia nervosa, in D. M. Garner and P. E. Garfinkel (eds.), *Handbook of psychotherapy for anorexia nervosa and bulimia* (New York: Guilford, 1985), p. 77.
5. For example, L. Weiss, M. A. Katzman, and S. Wolchik, *Treating bulimia: A psychoeducational approach* (Elmsford, NY: Pergamon, 1985).
6. For example, D. Hooker and E. Convisser, Women's eating problems: An analysis of a coping mechanism, *Personnel and Guidance Journal* 54 (1983): 236–239; N. Liss-Levinson, Disorders of desire: Women, sex, and food *Women and Therapy* 7 (1988): 121–129.
7. H. G. Lerner, *The dance of anger: A woman's guide to changing the patterns of intimate relationships* (New York: Perennial, 1986).
8. C. Tavris, *Anger: The misunderstood emotion* (New York: Simon and Schuster, 1982), p. 192. See also D. Frost and J. R. Averill, Differences between men and women in the everyday experience of anger, in J. R. Averill (ed.) *Anger and aggression: An essay on emotion* (New York: Springer-Verlag, 1982), pp. 281–316.
9. In a study using the Multidimensional Anger Inventory, men had *higher* scores than women on the anger-in dimension (feeling angry but not showing it). See J. M. Siegel, The Multidimensional Anger Inventory, *Journal of Personality and Social Psychology* 51 (1986): 191–200.
10. B. A. Kopper, Sex and sex-role differences in the experience and expression of anger (paper presented at the annual meeting of the American Psychological Association, New Orleans, 1989).
11. T. I. Rubin, *The angry book* (New York: Collier, 1970).
12. E. Harburg, E. H. Blakelock, and P. J. Roeper, Resentful and reflective coping with arbitrary authority and blood pressure, *Psychosomatic*

Medicine 41 (1978): 189–202; J. E. Dimsdale et al., Suppressed anger and blood pressure: The effects of race, sex, social class, obesity, and age, *Psychosomatic Medicine* 48 (1986): 430–436.

13. For a recent review of some research see J. M. Siegel, Anger and cardiovascular health, in H. S. Friedman (ed.), *Hostility coping and health* (Washington, D.C.: American Psychological Association, 1992), pp. 49–64.

14. C. Tavris, p. 20.

15. R. W. Novaco, *Anger control: The development and evaluation of an experimental treatment* Lexington, MA: Lexington, 1975).

16. D. D. Burns, *The feeling good handbook (New York: Plume, 1990).*

17. R. E. Alberti and M. L. Emmons, *Your perfect right: A guide to assertive behavior* (San Luis Obispo, CA: Impact, 1978), pp. 96–97.

Chapter 11

1. R. B. Stuart and B. Jacobson, *Weight, sex, and marriage: A delicate balance* (New York: Norton, 1987).

2. Ibid., p. 27.

3. R. S. Kalucy and A. H. Crisp, Some psychological and social implications of massive obesity, *Journal of Psychosomatic Research* 18 (1974): 465; P. Castelnuovo-Tedesco and D. Schiebel, Studies of superobesity: II. Psychiatric appraisal of jejunoileal bypass surgery, *American Journal of Psychiatry* 133 (1976): 26–31.

4. J. R. Marshall and J. Neill, The removal of a psychosomatic symptom: Effects on the marriage, *Family Process* 16 (1977): 273–280; J. R. Neill, J. R. Mashall, and C. E. Yale, Marital changes after intestinal bypass surgery, *Journal of the American Medical Association* 240 (1978): 447–450.

5. S. Catalano and E. E. Abramson, Weight loss and sexual behavior, *Journal of Obesity and Weight Regulation* 4 (1985): 268–273.

6. M. L. Glucksman, C. S. W. Rand, and A. J. Stunkard, Psychodynamics and obesity, *Journal of the American Academy of Psychoanalysis* 6 (1978): 103–115.

7. R. B. Stuart and B. Jacobson, p. 50.

8. C. S. Ford and F. A. Beach, *Patterns of sexual behavior* (New York: Harper & Row, 1951).